Islam and the West offer two very different and irreconcilable visions of society. The West currently faces huge challenges from the Islamic world. As Dr. Youssef points out in this book, Christians must view this conflict theologically and with a specific gospel focus. This book is an illuminating discussion of the times and of the challenges that Islam poses to the advance of the gospel. Let this book shape how you think, pray, and take the gospel to the ends of the earth.

—R. Albert Mohler, Jr.
President of The Southern Baptist Theological Seminary

THE
BARBARIANS
ARE HERE

THE BARBARIANS ARE HERE

PREVENTING THE COLLAPSE OF WESTERN
CIVILIZATION IN TIMES OF TERRORISM

MICHAEL YOUSSEF

WORTHY®
PUBLISHING

Published by Worthy Books, an imprint of Worthy Publishing Group, a division
of Worthy Media, Inc., One Franklin Park, 6100 Tower Circle, Suite 210,
Franklin, TN 37067.

Worthy is a registered trademark of Worthy Media, Inc.

HELPING PEOPLE EXPERIENCE THE HEART OF GOD
eBook available wherever digital books are sold.

Library of Congress Cataloging-in-Publication Data
Names: Youssef, Michael, author.
Title: The Barbarians are here : preventing the collapse of western
   civilization in times of terrorism / by Michael Youssef.
Description: Franklin, TN : Worthy Publishing, 2017. | Includes
   bibliographical references.
Identifiers: LCCN 2016055613 | ISBN 9781617956638 (hardcover)
Subjects: LCSH: Christianity and other religions--Islam. |
   Islam--Relations--Christianity. | Civilization, Western--Islamic
   influences. | Islamic fundamentalism. | Religious militants. |
   Terrorism--Religious aspects--Islam. | Civilization, Western--Forecasting.
Classification: LCC BP172 .Y68 2017 | DDC 261.2/7--dc23
LC record available at https://lccn.loc.gov/2016055613

Unless otherwise noted, all Scripture quotations are taken from The Holy Bible, New
International Version®, NIV® Copyright © 1973, 1978, 1984, 2011 by Biblica, Inc.®
Used by permission. All rights reserved worldwide.

Scripture quotations marked ESV are taken from the The Holy Bible, English Standard
Version, copyright © 2001 by Crossway Bibles, a publishing ministry of Good News
Publishers. Used by permission.

Quotations from the Quran are taken from the Abdullah Yusuf Ali translation (or, where
indicated, the Marmaduke Pickthall translation) in Three Translations of The Koran
(Al-Qur'an) Side by Side (public domain) at http://www.gutenberg.org/cache/epub/16955
/pg16955.html.

Published in association with Don Gates, The Gates Group, www.the-gates-group.com.

For foreign and subsidiary rights, contact rights@worthypublishing.com.

ISBN: 978-1-61795-663-8

Cover Design: Matt Smartt | Smartt Guys design

Printed in the United States of America
17 18 19 20 21 LBM 6 5 4 3 2 1

To all who are persecuted in the name of Christ around the world

CONTENTS

AUTHOR'S PREFACE

THOUGH I AM an American and a Christian, I was born in the Middle East and I grew up in a Muslim-dominated culture. I have a deep love and respect for the people of the Middle East, whether Christian, Jewish, or Muslim.

Please understand that the word *barbarians* in the title of this book refers to Islamist extremists and terrorists, not to Muslim people in general. This term has a specific meaning, which I discuss in greater detail in chapter 1. I use this term not as an insult or to hurt anyone's feelings, but because it is the most accurate term to describe a specific group of people who are not members of our Western civilization and who are actively trying to destroy our civilization from without and within.

It's important that we distinguish between Muslim ideology and Muslims as people. I do not shy away from speaking candidly about the impact of political Islam on the civilizations of the world. Yet I have many dear friends and acquaintances who embrace Islam, and I don't want anyone to misunderstand my genuine affection for Muslim people.

As a Christian, I see all other religious systems as fallen, broken, and unable to save. Jesus declared, "I am the way and the truth and the life. No one comes to the Father except through me" (John 14:6). The apostle Peter testified before the Sanhedrin, "Salvation is found in no one else, for there is no other name under heaven given to mankind by which we must be saved" (Acts 4:12). I would not be true to my Christian faith if I believed otherwise.

But the fact that I, as a Christian, view Islam as a false and fallen worldview does not mean I look down on Muslim people. In truth, I am compelled by my love for Muslim people. I deeply desire that Muslim people would experience the freedom and fullness of life that can be theirs through knowing Jesus Christ as their Lord and Savior.

1

TERRORISM—OUR EXILE

IN FEBRUARY 2015, ISIS released a horrifying five-minute video showing the beheading of twenty-one Coptic Christian men. The mass murder took place on the coast of Libya by the Mediterranean Sea. ISIS had kidnapped the men, all but one of whom were Egyptian, from the city of Sirte, Libya, where they were doing migrant work. Many of the men, dressed in orange jumpsuits like prisoners, spoke the name of the Lord Jesus as they were executed.

The one non-Egyptian martyr was a young man from West Africa, a coworker of the Egyptians. He was not a Christian at the time of the kidnapping, but when he saw the great faith of the Egyptian Christians, he received Jesus as his Lord and Savior. It is reported that when the terrorists told him he could live if he renounced Jesus, he replied, "Their God is my God."

The ISIS video was titled "A Message Signed with Blood to the Nations of the Cross." After the murders had been carried out, the hooded speaker pointed his knife to the sea, toward Rome, and declared in English, "We will conquer Rome by Allah's permission."[1]

The US government pretended not to know the terrorists' motives, referring to the twenty-one men not as martyred Christians but simply as "Egyptian citizens."[2] The terrorists, however, were obeying the commands of their "holy book." Quran 8.12 tells Muslims to terrorize "unbelievers" (Christians and Jews) and "smite ye above their necks" (that is, behead them). And Quran 47.4 commands Muslims who encounter "unbelievers" to "smite at their necks." So these Islamists beheaded twenty-one Christians and spilled their blood into the Mediterranean so that it might flow toward Rome—a declaration of war against the Vatican and the Christian West.

The Islamists intend to darken the Western world with the black flag of political Islam. Their goal is global conquest. They are inspired by ancient prophecies, such as this one, preserved in the Sunni hadith (traditions) by Abu Hurairah, a companion of Muhammad, the founder of Islam:

> [Armies carrying] black flags will come from Khurasaan [Iran and Afghanistan]. No power will be able to stop them and they will finally reach Eela [Baitul Maqdas,

the al-Aqsa Mosque in Jerusalem] where they will erect their flags.[3]

These Islamists are flooding into Western countries, often disguised as refugees. They are using our political system, legal system, and economic system against us. They are even using our compassion against us, preying on our generosity and our willingness to help people in need. Make no mistake: this is a gradual, deliberate invasion.

Is the notion of a conquered Western world and a global black-flag caliphate (Islamic empire) just a fevered Muslim dream? Or is it our worst nightmare in the making? With nearly fifty million Muslims already in Europe—many of whom are foot soldiers for the Islamic conquest—it's not as far-fetched as you might think. And Western governments are enabling the conquest in the name of compassion.

IMPORTING JIHAD

Since 2014, the governments of the European Union have been taking in huge numbers of Muslims from troubled and war-torn regions, including Syria, Afghanistan, Eritrea, Nigeria, and Somalia. Refugees have streamed into Spain and Italy from North Africa, into Greece via Turkey, and into Eastern Europe via the Balkans. Once inside the European Union, many spread out into France and England, Germany and Austria, and the Scandinavian countries. Some even take an Arctic route through Russia into Finland and Norway.

Many Western leaders, including Germany's chancellor, Angela Merkel, claim that their sole motivation for taking Muslim asylum seekers is humanitarian compassion. But there's a great deal of evidence that the real motivation is economic. Much as many American politicians (both Democrats and Republicans) quietly enable illegal immigration as a way of importing cheap labor, many European leaders see Muslim refugees as an exploitable class of low-wage workers. For short-term gain, they are selling out thousands of years of Judeo-Christian culture—and they are selling out the people they were elected to serve.

The cultural naïveté of many Westerners was captured in news photos I saw in the fall of 2015, in which groups of misguided Germans applauded trainloads of Islamist asylum seekers and held up signs reading "Welcome Refugees!" Meanwhile, the passengers emerging from the train—mostly young Arab men—raised their fists and shouted, "Allahu Akbar!" That shout—which means "Allah is great!"—is the Islamic shout of triumph and conquest. It is the shout that hordes of Islamists have raised throughout fourteen centuries of religious wars.

We have to wonder why so many Arab immigrants are young, healthy-looking men. You would expect that a refugee population from a war zone would consist largely of women and children. That is clearly not the case.

According to Eurostat, the official statistical analysis bureau of the European Union, men far outnumbered women among first-time asylum applicants in 2015. Among applicants aged fourteen to thirty-four, approximately 80 percent of applicants were male; among applicants aged thirty-five to sixty-four, approximately 66 percent were male. These are disturbing statistics. They show that European countries are importing large numbers of the key demographic group for Islamic terrorism—young Muslim men.[4]

Equally disturbing are the reports of some of the songs and slogans that many of these asylum seekers were singing and chanting as the refugee trains rolled into Europe: "May Allah make orphans out of their children." "May Allah make it difficult on their women." "Allah give victory to Islam everywhere." "Allahu Akbar! There is no god but Allah and the martyr is beloved by Allah!"[5]

And here's another troubling fact about Muslim refugee migration into the West: Christians make up 10 percent of the Syrian population, but only 2.5 percent of Syrian refugees. Of the 10,126 Syrian refugees who migrated to the United States in fiscal year 2016, only fifty-two (0.5 percent) were Christians.[6] Why are there so few Christian refugees? The answer to that question is a paradox: The ones with the most desperate need for refugee status are the least likely to obtain it. In the often-corrupt refugee programs of the United Nations, you need resources and connections to get help. Christians have no friends in Muslim-controlled high places and no money for bribes.

Christians avoid the refugee camps, where their lives would be in danger. Since the UN makes up asylum lists from refugee camp populations, Christians don't get counted. As Acton Institute scholar Jonathan Witt has concluded:

> As bad off as the Muslim refugees are, they aren't without politically well-connected advocates in the Middle East. Many Muslim powerbrokers are happy to see Europe and America seeded with Muslim immigrants. . . . By and large, they support Muslim immigration to the West and have little interest in seeing Christian refugees filling up any spaces that might have been filled by Muslim refugees.
>
> The deck, in other words, is heavily stacked against the Christian refugees.[7]

We also have to wonder why only Western countries are expected to take in refugees. Why aren't Arab countries taking in fellow Arabs? From a cultural standpoint, doesn't that make infinitely more sense than sending them into a non-Islamic culture where they don't know the language? Part of the answer lies in the fact that nations such as Saudi Arabia and Qatar are major sponsors of the expansionist, fundamentalist Wahhabi-Salafi school of Islam. Using refugees as an invasion strategy suits their purposes.

CONQUEST BY MIGRATION

There is an Islamic tradition—going back to the time of Islam's founder, Muhammad—known as *hijrah*, which literally means "migration."[8] In AD 622, Muhammad led his followers from Mecca to the city of Yathrib (now Medina). That migration was the first hijrah, and it transformed Muhammad into a political and military leader.

To this day, hijrah is one of the chief strategies for expanding Islam into other nations. Moving into a new land to spread Islam is viewed as an act of self-sacrifice that Allah will reward, according the Quran:

> He who forsakes his home in the cause of Allah, finds in the earth many a refuge, wide and spacious: Should he die as a refugee from home for Allah and His Messenger, His reward becomes due and sure with Allah. And Allah is Oft-Forgiving, Most Merciful. (4:100)

Many Muslim asylum seekers in Europe and America just want to escape persecution and war. But there can be no doubt that much of the Muslim migration is an act of hijrah—sometimes called "jihad by migration." So in a real sense, Western governments, including the United States, are importing jihad (struggle against "unbelievers") to our shores.

ISIS has published a troubling document called *Libya: The Strategic Gateway for the Islamic State*. The Quilliam Foundation, a British think tank, analyzed the document and called it a strategic plan to use Libya as the launch area for sending jihadists disguised as refugees into Europe. The document points out that Libya, located just three hundred miles from several European coasts, is well supplied with weapons from Muammar Gaddafi's arsenal. Libya, the document states, "has a long coast and looks upon the southern Crusader states, which can be reached with ease by even a rudimentary boat."[9] Many refugees have reached Europe by exactly that route.

In September 2015, a leading Islamic imam, Sheikh Muhammad Ayed, stood before a Muslim audience at Jerusalem's al-Aqsa Mosque, the third holiest site in the Islamic religion, and said, "We will breed children with them, because we shall conquer their countries, whether you like it or not, oh Germans, oh Americans, oh French, oh Italians, and all those like you. Take the refugees! We shall soon collect them in the name of the coming Caliphate."[10]

Western audiences were never intended to hear those

words, because they reveal the true aims of political Islam. They reveal the strategy that underlies the current invasion of Western civilization. Not all of those seeking asylum in the West are refugees.

Some have come as barbarians.

WHAT IS A BARBARIAN?

What is a *barbarian*? Why do I use this term to describe the Islamists who want to destroy us? This is not merely an exercise in name-calling or resorting to insults. I don't use the term *barbarian* to hurt anyone's feelings or to make someone out to be culturally inferior. This word has a specific meaning, and I am using it in a precise and careful way to convey a specific shade of significance.

A barbarian is a person who is not part of our civilization, who wants no part of our civilization, and who seeks the conquest and destruction of our civilization. The Islamists—Muslims who seek to restructure all governments and all of society in accordance with the laws of Islam—are cultural chauvinists who see Islam's Sharia law as vastly superior to Western secular law. They believe a totalitarian Islamic culture would be infinitely superior to the free societies of Western civilization, which are based on Judeo-Christian values. They seek the destruction of Western civilization, and that makes them—by definition—barbarians.

As Christians who seek to live in obedience to the Great Commission (the command of the Lord Jesus to preach the gospel to all people in every nation, recorded in Matthew 28:19–20), we want to convert people to a saving faith in Jesus Christ—*but only those who come willingly and freely*. Unlike the Islamist cult of the barbarians, Christians do not make converts at the point of the sword. We do not conquer in the name of Christ through murder, war, terror, and political subversion. That is one of the many differences between the Christian faith and the cult of the Islamists.

OVER THE DRAWBRIDGE AND ACROSS THE MOAT

For decades, Americans were vaguely aware that the Islamist barbarians were in the deserts of the Middle East, in the mountains of Afghanistan and Pakistan, and in the troubled Horn of Africa, destabilizing dictatorships, executing or enslaving "infidels," and raiding villages in countries with unpronounceable names. But the Muslim world seemed far away, remote, and irrelevant to our daily lives. Then came the 9/11 attacks—and everything changed.

On Monday night, September 10, 2001, Americans went to bed feeling safe, confident of the future, and invulnerable. On Tuesday morning, September 11, 2001, they woke up to a very different reality. The world had become a dangerous place, overshadowed by the smoke billowing from the mortally wounded towers of the World Trade Center. Without warning, America had become vulnerable to the rage of the barbarians.

Soon the terrorists were emerging out of nowhere, unleashing senseless death and destruction on our nation. A 2002 attack at Los Angeles International Airport killed two people and injured four others. In 2006, a Muslim extremist drove an SUV into a crowd of pedestrians in Chapel Hill, North Carolina, to "avenge the deaths of Muslims around the world."[11] Later that year, a Pakistani American shot six people, killing one, at a Jewish community center in Seattle. In 2009, a Muslim extremist killed a military recruiter and wounded another in Little Rock. Later that same year, a Muslim US Army psychiatrist opened fire on unarmed soldiers at Fort Hood, Texas, killing thirteen and wounding twenty-nine.

On April 15, 2013, the Boston Marathon was marred by a terror bombing that killed three (including an eight-year-old boy) and injured more than 260 people. The killers were two Islamist, Chechen brothers who had lived in the United States for more than a decade. The following year, an American-born convert to Islam carried out a gruesome hatchet attack on New York City police, who shot and killed him. In December 2015, two Islamists, a husband and wife, carried out a mass shooting at the Inland Regional Center in San Bernardino, California, where one of them was employed, leaving fourteen dead and twenty-two injured. In

June 2016, an American-born son of Afghan immigrants swore allegiance to ISIS and massacred forty-nine people in a gay nightclub in Orlando, Florida.

In 1982, when I wrote my first book, I considered calling it *The Barbarians Are Coming*. I could not write such a book today. It is far too late for such a title. The barbarians are not merely coming. They are *here*. They're over the drawbridge, across the moat, and within the city.

THE RISE OF ISLAM'S INFLUENCE

Today, the barbarians occupy our cultural citadels. They are inside every fortress of Western culture. Some of those who would tear down our civilization are in our legislatures, making laws. Some sit on our school boards. Some teach in our classrooms and lecture in our seminaries. Some even preach from our pulpits.

In October 2015, for example, First Community Church of Columbus, Ohio, invited Imam Feisal Abdul Rauf, founder of the Cordoba Initiative, to deliver a series of weekend lectures, including two Sunday morning services.[12] The name of the Cordoba Initiative is significant: Córdoba is a city in southern Spain where Muslim forces defeated Christian Spaniards in AD 711. The Moors called the city Qurtubah and turned the Catholic basilica into a mosque. The city did not return to Christian rule until the Reconquista in 1236. If the Cordoba Initiative is devoted to interfaith understanding, then why did Imam Rauf name his organization after the site of an Islamic conquest?

In June 2016, the Presbyterian Church (USA) held its 222nd General Assembly in Portland, Oregon, and asked Muslim community leader Wajidi Said to give the invocation. He prayed, "Lead us on the straight path—the path of all the prophets: Abraham, Ishmael, Isaac, Moses, Jesus and Muhammad."[13] Those who are familiar with the Quran know that this prayer was actually a subtly worded insult to Christians and Jews. It is drawn from the Fatihah, the opening chapter of the Quran, and is a commonly spoken prayer in Islam:

> Show us the straight path, the path of those whom Thou hast favoured; not the (path) of those who earn Thine anger nor of those who go astray. (Quran 1:006–007 Pickthall Translation)

Muslims understand "those who earn Thine anger" to be Jews and "those who go astray" to be Christians. The Presbyterians thought Wajidi Said prayed for interfaith understanding, but he actually invoked an insult against his Christian audience.

The barbarians are among us, and this is no mere accident of history. The Islamic religion was founded in the seventh century by Muhammad, and its goal has always been establishing a Muslim world empire, or global caliphate. Islam expanded rapidly under Umar ibn al-Khattab, Muhammad's chief disciple and the second caliph. Umar conquered most of the Byzantine Empire and all of Persia within a few years.

SPREAD BY THE SWORD

Islam didn't spread the way the Christian faith spread—by freewill evangelistic appeal. Islam was spread by the sword. It advanced as hordes of Islamic warriors conquered vast stretches of land across the Middle East, North Africa, and parts of Europe. The history of Islam and Christianity is filled with bloody struggle.

The armies of Islam swept up from North Africa to conquer much of the Iberian Peninsula (modern Spain). The Islamic armies would have advanced across Europe if they had not been defeated in 732 by the forces of Charles Martel at the Battle of Tours in north-central France. Historian Victor Davis Hanson called the Battle of Tours "a landmark battle that marked the high tide of the Muslim advance into Europe."[14] By the end of the tenth century, the Islamic Empire was in decline.

The religious-political-military system of Islam enjoyed a resurgence from the fifteenth to eighteenth centuries in the form of the Safavid dynasty in Iran, the Mughal dynasty in India, and the Ottoman Empire in Turkey. Islam conquered vast regions of Africa, Asia, and the Middle East.

Millions converted to Islam, either by choice or by subjugation. Constantinople, a fortress of Christianity, fell to the Ottomans in 1453 and became Istanbul, the Ottoman capital.

In Muslim-conquered lands, Christian boys were taken from their parents and reared as Muslims; then they were made to serve the armies of Islam. Christian churches became mosques. Islam continued its advance until 1683, when the Ottomans reached the center of Europe and laid siege to the gates of Vienna. The siege lasted two months.

On September 11, 1683, in the Battle of Vienna, defenders of the Holy Roman Empire under King John III Sobieski of Poland engaged and defeated the Ottomans. That day, the Ottoman Empire ceased to be a threat to Christendom. That victory saved Western civilization from destruction.

NOT-SO-ANCIENT HISTORY

That's ancient history, some say—yet many of the political struggles we see today are rooted in that time of Muslim invasions and Christian defensive stands. To this day, radical Islamists refer to the people of Western civilization as "Crusaders" (*al-Salibia*), and what we call "ancient history" is what many Islamists consider "current events."

Opponents of Christianity are quick to ask, "What about the crimes of the Crusades? What about the massacres the Crusaders conducted against Jewish and Muslim men, women, and children from the eleventh through fifteenth centuries?"

I don't defend the crimes committed by the Crusaders of the Middle Ages. Some of the leading Christian scholars of those times spoke out against the Crusades. The thirteenth-century Oxford friar Roger Bacon warned that all who suffered under the Crusades would become "more and more embittered against the Christian faith."[15]

Those who criticize the Crusades tend to ignore the most important part of the story: the Crusades were a reaction to more than four centuries of Islamic conquest. Historian Robert Louis Wilken observed, "By the middle of the eighth century more than fifty percent of the Christian world had fallen under Muslim rule."[16] The armies of Islam conquered cities that had once cradled the early church, including Antioch, Damascus, and Jerusalem. The Islamists obliterated the once-vital church of North Africa, which had once been home to such notable Christians as Augustine of Hippo and Cyprian of Carthage.

Opponents of Christianity need to be reminded that the Crusaders entered the fray not as aggressors but as defenders of a faith that was under siege by Muslim invaders. The Crusades were an attempt to turn back the tide of Islamic jihad and expansionism—a tide that still threatens Western civilization today.

THE ISLAMISTS' ADVANCE TO THE FUTURE

In the eighteenth, nineteenth, and twentieth centuries, the Islamic world was in decline—defeated at the Battle of Vienna, humiliated by European colonialism, and dominated militarily and economically by the West. But in the twenty-first century, Islam is advancing once more while Western civilization retreats. Though the Islamists once felt powerless against the West, they now feel empowered because of the Islamic takeover of Iran in 1979, the defeat of the Soviet Union in Afghanistan in 1988, the attacks of 9/11, and the rapid expansion and battlefield success of ISIS. Middle East oil wealth fuels their dreams of conquest.

Today, Islamic revivalists believe their ancient prophecies of a global caliphate are finally within reach. They see America as the Great Satan and jihad against Western civilization as a holy war. These barbarians have rejected civilized values. Everything we prize in the West—peace, freedom, knowledge, tolerance, human rights, and the worth of the individual—is scorned by political Islam.

Radical Islamists cite many reasons for hating our civilization. As we have seen, they call Americans "Crusaders" and identify us with Islam's European enemies during the Crusades, the religious wars of the eleventh through sixteenth centuries. They also remember how Western colonialists exploited the Arab world for its oil wealth. They hate the immorality in Hollywood movies and TV shows—and they blame that immorality on Christianity. They resent America's support for Israel. Most important of all, radical Islamists see the war between Islam and the West as a holy struggle against the forces of "unbelief."

The clash between civilization and barbarism has raged for centuries. We may have forgotten our history, but the Islamists have not forgotten theirs. They are still fighting a war that began in the seventh century AD. As twentieth-century philosopher George Santayana observed, "Those who cannot remember the past are condemned to repeat it."[17]

What is the past we are forgetting? What is the past we seem condemned to repeat?

HISTORY REPEATS ITSELF

We have heard it said many times: "History repeats itself." Is this merely a cliché? No, this is a profound biblical principle. As we read through the Bible, we see history repeating itself again and again.

We see the repetitive cycles of history most clearly in the book of Judges. The events in Judges take place over more than four centuries, beginning in about the fourteenth century before Christ. We see cycle after cycle in which (1) the people abandon God; (2) God delivers them over to the Canaanites, Moabites, Ammonites, Philistines, or other enemies; (3) the people repent and cry out to God for mercy;

and (4) God sends them a hero, a judge, who defeats the oppressor and delivers the people. Time passes, the people forget God's goodness, and the cycle repeats.

With each cycle, the people of Israel sink deeper into sin, idolatry, and rebellion. The pattern continues into the sixth century BC, a time that is depicted in several Old Testament books, including Jeremiah, 2 Kings, 2 Chronicles, Ezra, Nehemiah, and Daniel. These books depict the period of Jewish history known as the Babylonian Exile. In those days, Israel again became unfaithful to God, so God delivered the Israelites over to their enemies—in this case, the Babylonians.

The Babylonian king, Nebuchadnezzar, demanded tribute from the ruler of Judah, King Jehoiakim, who refused to pay. So Nebuchadnezzar sent his forces to lay siege to Jerusalem, resulting in Jehoiakim's death. This began a series of deportations, in which Nebuchadnezzar's army pillaged Jerusalem, destroyed its walls, and demolished the great temple of Solomon. Then the Babylonians led Jerusalem's nobility and leaders, along with much of the population of Judah, into exile in Babylon. Just as in the time of the judges, God took away His hand of protection from His people, and the exile began.

History repeats itself. This was true throughout Old Testament times, and it is still true today. When we are unfaithful and will not repent, God has no choice but to hand us over to our enemies to be shaken and oppressed. Only when we realize that we are reaping the just consequences of our sin do we cry out for deliverance. Only then will He rescue us from the oppressor. God has not repealed this principle. It remains in force today.

That's why I believe we are living in times like the era of the Judges and the era of Jeremiah. I'm convinced God has handed Western civilization over to our enemies. Who are the enemies of Western civilization? The barbarians, the radical Islamists, the violent jihadists, those who are still waging a religious war against the so-called Crusaders of the West.

OUR EXILE HAS BEGUN

Terrorism is our exile. The terrorists are our Babylonians.

Just as God handed over a rebellious and unfaithful Israel to the Babylonian Exile, God has handed over a rebellious and unfaithful Western culture—both our secular culture and our apostate church—to be shaken by terrorism, as Israel was shaken during their captivity in Babylon.

God has given us plenty of warning in His Word. We can read the Old Testament and see how God dealt with rebellious Israel in the past. Then we can look around us at our barbarian enemies, who have toppled our skyscrapers, murdered our soldiers and civilians, and attacked us when we were vulnerable.

We haven't learned the lessons of history. We have forgotten our past. And now we seem condemned to repeat it.

The barbarians are here. Our exile has begun. As our civilization rushes headlong toward collapse, it seems there is nothing we can do to avert catastrophe . . .

Or is there?

IT'S NOT TOO LATE

If I truly believed that nothing could be done to avert catastrophe, I wouldn't have written this book. It's not too late—not yet. Our civilization can still be rescued from inward collapse and barbarian invasion.

The cycle of unfaithfulness, exile, repentance, and deliverance goes all the way back to our first parents, Adam and Eve. They chose to go the wrong way, and they set in motion the cycle of rebellion and suffering that has echoed down through history. Now we in the Christian church, in Western civilization, and throughout the world are experiencing significant suffering as a result of Islamic terrorism.

Many naive souls believe that if we could reason with the terrorists, if we could improve economic conditions in the world, or if we could have better diplomacy and communication, then we could put an end to terrorism. But the problem is not a lack of diplomacy or economics. The Islamist barbarians who want to turn churches into mosques have no interest in anything we have to say. They want only our submission.

Some defenders of the Muslim religion have promoted

the false claim that *Islam* means "peace." Those who make this claim are counting on the Western ear being incapable of distinguishing between *Islam*—which derives from *aslama*, meaning "total surrender"—and *salaam*, the Arabic word for peace (as in, *As-salaam-alaikum*, a greeting that means "Peace be unto you"). The word *Islam* means "total surrender" because Islamic law requires unconditional submission. This word suggests all of Islam's opponents on their knees in surrender before the powerful, conquering Allah.

The Western secular perspective cannot understand the mind-set of the Islamists, who have been steeped in hatred of our faith and culture for fourteen hundred years. What we call "diplomacy" the Islamists call "weakness." They don't want to coexist with any other religion. They want to eliminate all religious competition.

Western civilization was founded by the Christian Reformation—a movement that brought light and life to a world emerging from the Dark Ages. But Western civilization has fallen away from its founding principles. So, as we will explore further in this book, we need a New Reformation to awaken the West from its slumber.

We who believe in the Lord Jesus Christ are not without hope. We have the greatest Hope of all. That Hope is the God-man, who hung on a cross to redeem humanity and who rose again to prove His divine power. Today, His arms are open wide and He calls to us, "Repent, come to Me, and

I will deliver you from your enemies and your exile, and I will restore you to wholeness."

The cycle that began with Adam and Eve, continued throughout Old Testament times, and remains in effect today can yet be broken. We are not doomed to destruction, even though the barbarians are already here. It's not too late.

But we haven't a moment to lose.

2

INVASION OF OTHER GODS

WHY IS THE THREAT of terrorism increasing in our nation and across Western civilization? Why is God displeased with the church? Why has He given us over to the terrorists, so that we will be afflicted by our enemies and disciplined by our exile and brought back to our senses? Why does God seem to have removed His hand of blessing and protection from our land?

It's because we have forsaken the Lord and have embraced other gods.

"IF MY PEOPLE..."

Christians often quote 2 Chronicles 7:14, which contains a beautiful promise that begins, "If my people, who are called by my name . . ." It's a wonderful promise—but we shouldn't forget the *context* of that promise.

Soon after King Solomon had constructed the temple in Jerusalem, the Lord spoke to him:

> I have heard your prayer and have chosen this place for myself as a temple for sacrifices.
>
> When I shut up the heavens so that there is no rain, or command locusts to devour the land or send a plague among my people, if my people, who are called by my name, will humble themselves and pray and seek my face and turn from their wicked ways, then I will hear from heaven, and I will forgive their sin and will heal their land. . . .
>
> But if you turn away and forsake the decrees and commands I have given you and go off to serve other gods and worship them, then I will uproot Israel from my land, which I have given them, and will reject this temple I have consecrated for my Name. I will make it a byword and an object of ridicule among all peoples. This temple will become a heap of rubble. All who pass by will be appalled and say, "Why has the Lord done such a thing to this land and to this temple?" People will answer, "Because they have forsaken the Lord, the God of their ancestors, who brought them out of Egypt, and have embraced other

gods, worshiping and serving them—that is why he brought all this disaster on them." (2 Chronicles 7:12–14, 19–22)

Yes, God has promised to heal our land if we turn to Him, humble ourselves, pray, and turn from our wicked ways. But God also promised that if we are unfaithful to Him, if we serve other gods and worship them, then He will bring disaster upon us.

We don't like to admit that the calamities shaking our civilization might be the result of our own sin. We like to point fingers of blame at non-Christians. We like to rail against abortion and sexual depravity because those are not (generally speaking) the sins of the church. The church does not operate abortion mills, pornography websites, or houses of prostitution. Our hands are clean—aren't they?

But what if the abortion and sexual depravity in our culture are not so much the *causes* of the decline of Western civilization as symptoms of a deeper sickness? God has promised that if we in the church would repent of our sin and turn back to God, then He would heal our land. Perhaps if the church turned away from its apostasy, God would heal our civilization of abortion and sexual depravity—and of the debt that will soon collapse our economy; and of the lies, bribery, influence peddling, and corruption of our public officials; and of the racial strife that is dividing our society;

and of the violence that is destroying our communities.

If we in the church would humble ourselves and repent of our sins, I believe God would lead us out of our Babylonian Exile and deliver us from the threat of terrorism.

THE SINS OF THE CHURCH

What, then, should we repent of? What are the sins of the church?

They are the same sins Israel committed in the Old Testament—sins of spiritual adultery, of unfaithfulness to God and His Word. As Ezekiel prophesied against Israel:

> In the nations where they have been carried captive, those who escape will remember me—how I have been grieved by their adulterous hearts, which have turned away from me, and by their eyes, which have lusted after their idols. They will loathe themselves for the evil they have done and for all their detestable practices. (Ezekiel 6:9)

You may say, "But I love God. I go to church faithfully. How am I guilty of spiritual adultery? When have I lusted after idols?"

These are the same questions unfaithful Israel asked before God's judgment fell upon the nation. God told Israel through the prophet Hosea, "The people have broken my covenant and rebelled against my law." But the people cried out in protest, "Our God, we acknowledge you!" God replied, "Israel has rejected what is good; an enemy will pursue him. They set up kings without my consent; they choose princes without my approval. With their silver and gold they make idols for themselves to their own destruction. . . . They sow the wind and reap the whirlwind" (Hosea 8:1–7).

The people thought they knew God and acknowledged Him, yet God replied that Israel had rejected God's will and had chased after false gods—and as a result of their unfaithfulness, an enemy would pursue them.

We have to ask ourselves: "How have we, as Christians in the twenty-first century, been unfaithful to God?"

Answer: by adding to—and taking away from—the crystal-clear purity of God's Word.

AN ADULTERATED FAITH

The unfaithful Israelites did not abandon the Hebrew religion. They still made the ritual sacrifices in the temple, as required by the Law of Moses. But they added false religion to their worship of God. They sacrificed to the pagan gods as well as to the one true God.

Many in the church today commit the same sin. The apostle Paul warned the church in Corinth:

I am jealous for you with a godly jealousy. I promised you to one husband, to Christ, so that I might present you as a pure virgin to him. But I am afraid that just as Eve was deceived by the serpent's cunning, your minds may somehow be led astray from your sincere and pure devotion to Christ. For if someone comes to you and preaches a Jesus other than the Jesus we preached, or if you receive a different spirit from the Spirit you received, or a different gospel from the one you accepted, you put up with it easily enough. (2 Corinthians 11:2–4)

Paul used symbolism identical to that which God had used when speaking through the prophets Ezekiel and Hosea: both Israel and the church are pictured as a wife who commits adultery and prostitutes herself by adding falsehood to the pure truth of God's Word. Paul came to the Corinthians preaching a pure devotion to Christ—yet when a false teacher came into their midst, teaching false notions of Christ and the gospel, the Corinthians listened to his lies and added his false teachings to God's truth.

Where Paul said he feared the Corinthians would be seduced away from a "sincere and pure devotion to Christ," the word "sincere" is not the best translation. The Greek word is *haplotēs*, which literally means singleness and simplicity[1]—

a word that would describe a glass of clear water with no impurities or additives. It's interesting that both the Old Testament prophets and the apostle Paul use the image of *adultery* to describe religion to which falsehood has been added. Similarly, we say that when a harmful substance is added to pure water, the water has been *adulterated*. To adulterate is to contaminate.

The Western church has adulterated the gospel. The good news of Jesus Christ is simple and clear—yet we have clouded and adulterated it with false philosophies, ideologies, and doctrines. We have added business principles, psychological principles, worldly philosophies, "new revelations," political ideologies, and human greed to the purity of the gospel message. Then we call this poisonous stew "Christianity."

Oh, we have not denied Jesus. We love Jesus. We sing songs about Jesus. We preach sermons about Jesus. We've just added a few "harmless" ideas to make Jesus more "relevant." We forget that the people of Israel did not deny God either. They still proclaimed their love for God, and they still offered sacrifices to Him. They just added a few "harmless" idols and practices borrowed from the Canaanites and the Philistines—to make God more "relevant."

In His High Priestly Prayer before going to the cross, Jesus prayed, "Sanctify them by the truth; your word is truth"

(John 17:17). But when we adulterate God's Word with false teachings from the surrounding culture, the Word ceases to be truth. We cannot be sanctified by adulterated "truth."

The apostle James warned the first-century church (and the twenty-first-century church):

> You adulterous people, don't you know that friendship with the world means enmity against God? Therefore, anyone who chooses to be a friend of the world becomes an enemy of God. Or do you think Scripture says without reason that he jealously longs for the spirit he has caused to dwell in us? (James 4:4–5)

When we blend worldly philosophies and ideologies with the gospel, we are practicing friendship with the world—and making ourselves enemies of God.

CONTAMINATED CHRISTIANITY

A number of church movements and fads have emphasized practices not found in Scripture. These practices are given various names, such as "holy laughter," "soaking prayer," "prayer labyrinths," being "slain in the Spirit," and on and on. One leading advocate of such extrabiblical practices rationalizes, "I believe it's possible for us to recover realms of anointing, realms of insight, realms of God that have been untended for decades simply by choosing to reclaim them and perpetuate them for future generations."[2]

One of the practices this man advocates is what he calls "grave sucking" or "mantle grabbing." This practice stems from a false belief, without biblical foundation, that the empowerment of God's Spirit resides in the dead bones of believers who have passed on. This man claims a believer can lay hands on the headstone or prostrate himself upon the grave of a departed saint, and God will transfer a spiritual "anointing" from the corpse to the believer. Such "realms of anointing" as this come not from Scripture but from the human imagination. God warns repeatedly against contaminating His truth with such wild notions.

Some people, on both the political Left and the political Right, have contaminated the Christian faith with contemporary political ideologies. It's not enough for them to simply preach Christ and Christ crucified (1 Corinthians 1:23). Jesus affirmed that we should be engaged as good citizens, rendering unto Caesar what is Caesar's and unto God what is God's (Matthew 22:21). In other words, we should do our civic duty toward the government, obeying the law, paying taxes, casting an informed vote, and so forth. Yet we also need to be careful not to pollute the gospel with worldly political ideologies of either the Left or the Right.

Social Gospel

In the hope of creating a utopia on earth, some on the religious Left have added progressive political ideas to the gospel, producing a political caricature they call the Social Gospel. This "gospel" is not the good news that Jesus died to save us but the notion that Christian compassion demands that we provide a welfare state with universal health care, affirmative action, and open borders. An extreme form of the Social Gospel called Liberation Theology combines the failed economic theories of Karl Marx with selected teachings of Christ.

While we have a Christian duty to oppose injustice and immorality—abortion, homosexuality, pornography, and other forms of depravity in our culture—political action can never take the place of the good news. We will never create a utopia on earth by legislating a conservative social agenda. God's way of changing society has always involved preaching the good news of salvation—changing one heart at a time through the pure gospel.

Many Christians on both the Right and the Left have lost faith in the power of the gospel to change hearts—and to change society. So instead of preaching the gospel, we have tried to *force* change on society through political power. We've tried to change laws instead of hearts. But as Jeremiah warns, "This is what the LORD says: 'Cursed is the one who trusts in man, who draws strength from mere flesh and whose heart turns away from the LORD'" (Jeremiah 17:5).

Prosperity Gospel

Another way we have adulterated God's Word is through the so-called Prosperity Gospel. This is the notion that God wants every believer to be financially prosperous and that the way to receive God's blessings of worldly wealth involves increasing our faith and donating to Prosperity Gospel preachers. These notions originated in the nineteenth-century New Thought movement, which claimed that the mind has hidden power to make us healthy and wealthy. The New Thought movement gave rise to many Mind Science cults, such as Christian Science, Religious Science, Science of Mind—and the Prosperity Gospel.

What does Jesus think of the Prosperity Gospel? In Luke 12:15, He said, "Watch out! Be on your guard against all kinds of greed; life does not consist in an abundance of possessions." Then Jesus told about a man who amassed great wealth—but as he celebrated his good fortune, God said, "You fool! This very night your life will be demanded from you. Then who will get what you have prepared for yourself?" Jesus concluded, "This is how it will be with whoever stores up things for themselves but is not rich toward God" (Luke 12:20–21).

The Prosperity Gospel promotes greed and a lack of compassion for the poor. It says, "If you are poor or sick, it's your fault." Bible teacher David Jackman recalls an African pastor he once met. This pastor went to serve in a West African church, but the people of the church had been steeped in the Prosperity Gospel. They saw this pastor in his old clothes, driving a beat-up car—and they told him he could not be a true man of God because God had not blessed him with wealth. So they fired him.[3]

Emerging Church

Another false gospel is a postmodern movement called the Emerging Church. This movement largely attracts undiscerning young people. Many leaders of the Emerging Church preach universalism: the notion that there is no hell, no judgment, no need for forgiveness, and ultimately, no need for a Savior. It treats the great historic certainties of the Christian faith—the virgin birth, the miracles of Jesus, His death and resurrection and promised return—as mere narratives, allegories, or fables from which we derive comfort.

In the Emerging Church, preaching the gospel as absolute truth is viewed as dogmatic and didactic. So the Emerging Church has replaced sound biblical doctrine with a "post-evangelical narrative." In denying the reality of hell, the false teachers of the Emerging Church are only helping to increase the population of hell.

One book by an Emerging Church leader laments the fact that, down through history, orthodox Christianity has "shown a pervasive disdain for other religions of the world." He goes on to list several religions, including Buddhism, Hinduism, and atheism, that orthodox Christians should view "not as enemies but as beloved neighbors, and whenever possible, as dialogue partners and even collaborators."[4]

Yet God's great indictment against Israel was that the Israelites willingly became "dialogue partners" and "collaborators" with the religions of the Canaanites and Phoenicians, the Egyptians and Assyrians, and the Persians and the Babylonians. Though God had told Israel, "You shall have no other gods before me" (Exodus 20:3), the people repeatedly turned to idols and false religions—and that is why God sent them into exile in Babylon (2 Kings 17:7–23). Israel was punished and exiled for doing *exactly* what the leaders of the Emerging Church advocate today.

I'm not saying we should view Buddhists, Muslims, Hindus, or atheists as enemies. We mustn't hate them. We must love them with the love of Jesus Christ. But the only way to *authentically* love them is by sharing the gospel with them. Collaborating with false teachers might win friendship with the world, but it would betray the One who declared, "I am the way and the truth and the life. No one comes to the Father except through me" (John 14:6).

The notion that Christians ought to mingle biblical truth

with the falsehoods of other religions is spiritual poison. Like the cyanide-laced Kool-Aid served at the cult compound of Jonestown, the Emerging Church version of Christianity is a suicide potion. Millions of earnest young people are drinking the Emerging Church Kool-Aid, unaware that they are drinking to their own spiritual death. They think they have discovered an exciting new form of Christianity, but it's the same old deception that led the Israelites into slavery and exile.

Once you set your sights on friendship with the world, you place yourself in spiritual jeopardy. If the praise of unbelievers is what you want, then it's not hard to get. Simply compromise the truth. Unbelievers will tell you, "We love your uncertainty, ambiguity, doubt, and tolerance of other religions. Just do away with your claim that Jesus is 'the way and the truth and the life,' and let's agree that all paths lead to God."

But Jesus never said, "Tolerance for other religions will set you free," or, "Doubt will set you free," or, "Uncertainty will set you free." Jesus said, "If you hold to my teaching, you are really my disciples. Then you will know the truth, *and the truth will set you free*" (John 8:31–32; emphasis added). Truth comes from the teachings of Jesus, and only the truth of Jesus will set us free.

The Emerging Church asks the same question Pontius

Pilate asked before handing Jesus over to the bloodthirsty crowd: "What is truth?" (John 18:38). Jesus saw the dismissive attitude behind Pilate's question, and He refused to answer. During His earthly ministry, Jesus taught His disciples the importance of knowing the truth and speaking the truth and defending the truth. Jesus is Truth incarnate.

Other False Gospels

Of course, there are many other false gospels spreading heresies and apostasy in our culture—more than I can discuss in detail. For example, there's the Therapeutic Gospel, which tells us that Jesus came to make us mentally well-adjusted and happy, and to help us reach our potential. There's the Formal Church Gospel, which says that if we follow certain church rules and rituals, if we are baptized as infants and confirmed in the church, then we are "saved."

There's the Moral Gospel, which says that if we live a good life and we're nice to people, and our good deeds outweigh our bad deeds, we'll earn a place in heaven. There's the No-Judgment Gospel, which says that a loving God would never send anyone to hell, so there's nothing to worry about and no need to evangelize the world—everyone gets saved in the end.

There's the God-Is-Everywhere Gospel, which says, "I don't need to believe in Jesus or the cross for the resurrection.

I don't need the Bible. I don't need the church. Nature is my church. I don't need to be saved. I'm not religious—I'm spiritual." There's the All-Paths-Lead-to-God Gospel, which says that whether we are Christian, Jewish, Hindu, Buddhist, Wiccan, or Muslim, we'll all reach the same destination (in complete denial of John 14:6). And there's the Self-Help Motivational Gospel, which says that Jesus came to give us a positive outlook on life—we don't need to be saved, just motivated!

TWENTY-FIRST-CENTURY IDOLATRY

Some would have us believe that the Christian faith contains some truths, other religions contain other truths, and if we put these truths together and all sing "Kumbaya," we'll have a more complete truth. That is twenty-first-century idolatry.

The Israelites, before the Babylonian Exile, practiced a similar approach to truth. They believed God had delivered some truth through Moses, but they also wanted to sample the "truth" of the Canaanites and the other false religions around them.

God made it clear to Israel that there are not many paths to God; there is only one way.

And God's message to us hasn't changed. It remains the same: Do not tamper with the truth of God. The fate of those who adulterate the gospel is the same today as it was in ancient Israel: *exile.*

SEDUCED INTO SPIRITUAL ADULTERY

A theologian at Union Theological Seminary in New York has written a book called *Without Buddha I Could Not Be a Christian*. As you read his explanation of what it means to be a "Buddhist Christian," you realize that in order to add Buddhism to his belief system, he had to subtract all that is essentially Christian from his "Christianity."

For example, he wrote about his "queasiness about the resurrection of Jesus" and tried to make the case that early Christians didn't actually believe in a literal resurrection. He asked, "Might the past reality, and present meaning and power, of the 'resurrection' be something much bigger than what we have been taught about Jesus stepping out of the tomb and talking with his followers? Might the resurrection be a symbol of something that is much different from and deeper than the miracle of the dead person brought back to life?"[5]

In short, this theologian is denying the core truths of the gospel, the essence of what it means to believe in Christ. He went on to make this startling claim: "As far as we can tell, Jesus never really called himself the Son of God or claimed divinity. That came later, after his death."[6] It's hard to believe that a seminary theologian could be unaware of the many times Jesus referred to God as His Father and Himself as the Son. When Simon Peter told Jesus, "You are the Messiah, the Son of the living God," Jesus did not contradict him—He said, "Blessed are you, Simon son of Jonah, for this was not revealed to you by flesh and blood, but by my Father in heaven" (Matthew 16:16–17). As for claiming divinity, Jesus said, "I and the Father are one" (John 10:30).

You cannot add Buddhism to Christianity without eviscerating Christianity. You have to slice Christianity open, rip out its core truths, and throw them on the ash heap in order to make room for the tenets of Eastern religion. By doing so, you may make friends with the world—but at the expense of God's truth. If you say, "Without Buddha I could not be a Christian," you are actually saying, "There is something lacking in Jesus. The teachings of Jesus, the death of Jesus, and the resurrection of Jesus are not enough. I need to add an idol, another religion from the surrounding culture, in order to make Jesus complete." That is spiritual adultery.

More than three decades ago, Dr. Francis A. Schaeffer predicted that large parts of the Christian world, including much of evangelical Christianity, would be seduced into spiritual adultery—and that the results would be devastating:

A large segment of the evangelical world has become seduced by the world spirit of this present age. And more than that, we can expect the future to be a further disaster if the evangelical world does not take a stand for biblical truth and morality in the full spectrum of life. *For the evangelical accommodation to the world of our age represents the last barrier against the breakdown of our culture.* And with the final removal of this barrier will come social chaos and the rise of authoritarianism in some form to restore social order.[7]

Dr. Schaeffer was a remarkably perceptive futurist. He realized that spiritual defection in the church would affect not merely the church. The defection of the church from God's truth would also remove the barriers that restrain evil and disorder in society. As crime, civil unrest, and barbaric acts of terrorism rise, the people panic—and they demand authoritarian government to restore the order that vanished when the moral authority of the church collapsed.

When the church no longer proclaims God's truth, when Christians are no longer salt and light, the world becomes ripe for authoritarian, totalitarian government. The people will beg for a strongman leader—even a dictator—who promises safety, security, and order. And conditions will be ripe for the rise of the Antichrist.

You might say, "I would never willingly accept the kind of authoritarian government that Francis Schaeffer predicted." But the truth is, you already have.

After the attacks of 9/11, the American people became much more accepting of authoritarian measures, including humiliating pat-down searches at airports. We surrender our Fourth Amendment rights whenever we submit to a TSA search. We now have metal detectors and security guards at the entrances to every major public building—and even at many public schools. The government can easily monitor our emails, phone calls, and computer searches—and the American people do not protest. Wherever we go out in public, we are scanned by security cameras. Mountains of data on our buying habits, our whereabouts, and the views we express on social media are being permanently stored on government servers.

The authoritarianism Francis Schaeffer predicted is already here—and it's increasing. The next time America suffers a 9/11-scale attack, we can expect the government to clamp down hard on our freedoms. A sufficiently devastating attack might even lead the government to suspend the Constitution altogether.

The rise of the authoritarian state can be traced directly to our failure as Christians to take a bold and uncompromising stand for biblical truth and morality. The gradual loss of our freedom and privacy in the face of growing terrorism is added proof that we are living in a time of exile—and we have brought the exile of terrorism upon ourselves.

None of us can escape responsibility for the future of our civilization. We must all make godly choices right now, today—or we will condemn ourselves, our children, and our grandchildren to a long, horrifying night of exile.

3

THE BARBARIAN INVASION

IT WAS NEW YEAR'S EVE, and all across Germany, revelers gathered in the streets to greet the coming of 2016. Past celebrations had always been peaceful and safe. The crowds of German people, especially women, were unprepared for the danger all around them. In the great cities of Germany—Cologne, Hamburg, Frankfurt, Dortmund, Düsseldorf, Stuttgart, and Bielefeld—the barbarians hunted their victims. There were similar attacks against women in Austria, Switzerland, and Finland.

Roving packs of young men, described as Arab or North African in appearance, moved through the crowds, communicating with one another with smartphones, targeting female victims. Typically, twenty or thirty men would surround a single victim or a group of victims. In some cases, they would attack a woman walking with her husband or boyfriend.

It was cold on New Year's Eve, and victims were dressed in heavy winter clothes, yet the men reached inside the victims' clothing, groping and pulling off clothes, stealing phones and purses—and in some cases, throwing victims to the ground and raping them.

"We tried to fight off their hands," said one young woman. "Everywhere I looked, I saw girls crying." A woman named Sara sought help from the police, to no avail. "I never experienced that a policeman says, 'I would love to help you, but I can't,'" she said. An eighteen-year-old victim named Johanna recalled, "I was grabbed continually. . . . [It was] the worst night of my life." One sexual assault victim was an on-duty policewoman in Cologne.

Another young woman from Cologne, named Jenny, suffered serious burns after an attacker shoved a burning firecracker into her coat. She recalled, "I heard a sizzling sound. . . . [I] tried to get the firecracker out of the hood. Then it fell into my jacket and burned everything. . . . The scars will be permanent. I was lucky it didn't explode."[1]

Police estimated that at least two thousand foreign men were involved in the attacks. Police in Cologne arrested 153 suspects, only four of whom were German citizens. Many were recently arrived illegal immigrants or "asylum seekers," men who had been welcomed to Germany as refugees from war-torn Islamic countries. In February 2015, ISIS announced a plan to send half a million refugees to Europe and America, with many ISIS fighters among them.

The pro-immigrant mayor of Cologne, Henriette Reker, suggested that the attacks were merely a cultural misunderstanding. "We will also have to explain our Carnival better to people from other cultures," she told reporters, "so that there's no confusion about the cheerful behavior in Cologne that has nothing to do with candor, especially candid sexuality."[2] But the mass abuse of women by Muslim men had nothing to do with "confusion." It's simply foolish to try to persuade barbarians to behave in a civilized way.

Those men were not confused. They were Islamist barbarians who knew what they were doing. It was a sophisticated and deliberate mass attack, coordinated on social media. Pakistani journalist Shamil Shams, himself a Muslim, wrote an opinion piece at Germany's Deutsche Welle website, saying:

I am a person from a Muslim background who has been living in Germany for many years, and have always been treated with respect and humility. I have always felt safer in Germany than in Pakistan. . . . What happened in Cologne happens regularly in my homeland, Pakistan. The men are never ashamed, never feel guilty, never show remorse about the way they treat women in that part of the world.

The men who sexually harassed girls in Cologne were not demented; they knew what they were doing. And I am sure they did it with absolute contempt for the European culture, its norms and its people.[3]

German feminist Alice Schwarzer, editor of *Emma* magazine, has broken the feminist conspiracy of silence around these attacks. She told Emma-Kate Symons of Women in the World, "Many feminists have remained silent from the outset regarding the problem of Islamist agitation, out of fear they will be accused of racism. . . . Violence is always the dark core of domination, whether it is between ethnic groups, or between different peoples or between the sexes. . . . In Germany we have never seen this before: mass sexual violence in public with a powerless police looking on. This is a whole new dimension."

Schwarzer added that the New Year's Eve attacks in Germany and other countries were "no coincidence. This is organized. . . . I'm not talking about Muslims, or Islam as a faith. I'm talking about the politicization of Islam . . . whose banner is the veiling of women. This started in Iran in 1979 with Khomeini, and [elsewhere] it has been financed by Saudi Arabia. The Islamists firmly established themselves in Afghanistan and Chechnya . . . and are now . . . arriving triumphant in the heart of Europe."[4]

Another feminist, French Egyptian author Sérénade Chafik, called the New Year's Eve assaults "sexual terrorism." She knows radical political Islam all too well; her book *Repudiation* describes her life during the violent reign of Sharia law in Egypt. She said that the New Year's Eve attacks reminded her of the rape of female protesters during the Arab Spring uprisings in Cairo's Tahrir Square.

"This is sexual terrorism directed towards women," she told Women in the World. These young Muslim extremists, she said, employ a disturbing Middle Eastern concept of "*honor 'a l'Oriental,*' in which the honor of a family, a tribe, or even a nation is found between women's legs"—and these barbarians seek to defile that honor by sexually assaulting the women of that family, tribe, or nation. The act of rape, she says, "will thus destroy the honor of these nations and humiliate not only women but Western countries. . . . The Islamists are at war with the West. And sexual violence was always a war strategy. So they decided to hit two birds with the one stone: striking women, and humiliating men who cannot protect their 'own' women."[5]

These are the ruthless tactics of barbarians. They are among us. They are at war with us whether we like it or not—and whether we realize it or not.

THE DUSTBIN OF HISTORY

We have seen the unmistakable parallels between Western civilization today and Israel in the days leading up to the Babylonian captivity. There are equally striking parallels between America today and the fall of the Roman Empire. Because history tends to repeat itself, it's wise to look back over history to see if there are echoes of the past in our own time, our own culture. If we are honestly paying attention to the lessons of history, we have to acknowledge that, yes, there are echoes of both the fall of ancient Israel and the fall of ancient Rome in our society today.

The historical parallels between the collapse of Rome and the current decline of America should chill us to the bone. The fall of Rome was not the result of just one or two factors, but of many factors that conspired to collapse the Roman civilization—much as we now see an array of factors undermining our own civilization. In fact, most of the factors that destroyed the Roman Empire are already metastasizing in our culture today.

Barbarian invasions delivered the deathblow to the Roman Empire. But long before the barbarians arrived to pillage and plunder, Rome was crumbling from within. Barbarians could not have destroyed Rome from the outside if the Romans hadn't already weakened their own civilization. The following factors caused the fall of Rome:

1. *The Romans entertained themselves to death.* In the Roman world, as in today's American culture, the more violent the entertainment, the better.

2. *Political corruption was rampant.* In Rome, as in America today, politicians viewed political office not as a public service but as a road to riches. Roman senators served the special interests, not the citizens of Rome.

3. *Rome was in a state of continual war.* Foreign wars distracted the Roman people from domestic problems but, as in America today, the military conflicts took a heavy toll in blood and treasure. Historian Evan Andrews wrote, "Even as Rome was under attack from outside forces, it was also crumbling from within. . . . Constant wars and overspending had significantly lightened imperial coffers."[6]

4. *Rome could not sustain its war effort without mercenaries.* The Roman Empire hired so many Germanic mercenaries, Andrews observed, "that Romans began using the Latin word 'barbarus' in place of 'soldier.'. . . Many of the barbarians who sacked the city of Rome and brought down the Western Empire had earned their military stripes while serving in the Roman legions."[7] Today's mercenaries are military contractors such as Blackwater and DynCorp.

5. *Rome's middle class was economically crushed.* The Roman Empire conquered nations and brought back slaves— and slave labor reduced wages for the common people. The

Roman economy became dependent on slave labor. Illegal immigrants are the "slave labor" force of the American economy today.

6. *Rome could not control its borders*, much like modern-day America. The Roman Empire became vast, unmanageable, and practically borderless. The "illegal immigrants" of Roman times included the Visigoths, Franks, Vandals, and Arabs. Historians Will and Ariel Durant observed:

> If Rome had not engulfed so many men of alien blood in so brief a time, if she had passed all these newcomers through her schools instead of her slums, if she had treated them as men with a hundred potential excellences, if she had occasionally closed her gates to let assimilation catch up with infiltration, she might have gained new racial and literary vitality from the infusion, and might have remained a Roman Rome, the voice and citadel of the West. The task was too great.[8]

7. *Moral decay hastened the death of Rome*, just as immorality is destroying America today. Emperor Trajan, who ruled from AD 98 to 117, presided over the most prosperous time in Roman history, yet historian Edward McNall Burns noted that, according to records from that time, "there were 32,000 prostitutes in Rome during the reign of Trajan,

and . . . homosexuality was exceedingly common and even fashionable."[9]

Salvian, a fifth-century Roman Christian writer, observed that the Vandals, a small barbarian tribe from the north, had conquered Roman Spain as God's judgment against the immorality of the Roman culture:

> The barbarians are now cleansing by chastity those lands which the Romans polluted by fornication. . . . God gave all [of Spain] to the weakest enemies to show that it was not the strength of numbers but the cause that conquered. . . . We are right now being overcome solely by the impurity of our vices. . . .
>
> I ask: What hope of pardon or of life can there be for us in the sight of God when we see chastity among the barbarians and are, ourselves, unchaste? I say: Let us be ashamed and confused. . . .
>
> You, O Roman people, be ashamed; be ashamed of your lives.[10]

This warning from ancient Rome applies to our lives today. We think that the terrorists and jihadists are too weak, too few in number, or too far away to overcome our great nation. As 9/11 recedes in our collective memory, Americans have become complacent, and even arrogant. We don't think 9/11—or something worse—could ever happen here again.

In January 2014, the *New Yorker* interviewed the American president, who dismissed the threat of the terror group ISIS, saying, "If a jayvee [junior varsity] team puts on Lakers uniforms that doesn't make them Kobe Bryant." Six months later, that "jayvee team" declared itself a global caliphate. Within two years, it had conquered a vast region in Iraq and Syria, and dominated the lives of some eight million people. And by mid-2016, it had killed hundreds of people in terror attacks in France, Belgium, Turkey, Lebanon, Tunisia, Yemen, and Afghanistan—and had brought down a Russian airliner over the Sinai Peninsula. ISIS also inspired attacks in Boston, San Bernardino, and Orlando, resulting in scores of American deaths.

The barbarian invasion of Western civilization has begun. And it will intensify. Like the Roman Empire, we have weakened our civilization from within—and now we are being invaded from without. If this pattern continues, we can expect history to repeat itself. We can expect to see the fall of the American Empire and the collapse of Western civilization.

Historian Niall Ferguson is a distinguished professor of history at Harvard and a senior research fellow at Oxford and Stanford universities. He has observed that when civilizations die, they do not decline gradually. They collapse suddenly. Though the Roman Empire stood for five hundred years, it fell, wrote Ferguson, "within the span of a single generation."

Civilizations can appear healthy for years—then topple with astonishing suddenness.[11]

The fall of Israel took place exactly as Ferguson describes. After decades of moral decline, the end came swiftly—and the people were led into slavery in Babylon. Would God send us into exile the same way? Perhaps our exile has already begun. As mentioned earlier, I am convinced that terrorism *is* our exile.

There is a price to pay for sin. There is a price to pay for adulterating God's truth. There is a price to pay for ignoring God's truth. If we don't turn back to God and stand firmly on His truth, then our children and grandchildren will pay the price.

THE NEW DARK AGES

The world—and especially Western civilization—could experience a moral, intellectual, political, and economic renaissance if God's people, who are called by His name, would turn back to God and His Word (2 Chronicles 7:14). I know this is possible because it has happened before.

We live in a time of moral and spiritual anarchy, when the Christian church has added so many false ideas and unbiblical notions to the gospel that the good news of Jesus Christ has become obscured and unrecognizable. These are the conditions that prevailed in the first Dark Ages, from the fall of Rome to the Protestant Reformation, from the fifth century to the early sixteenth century. During those days, as in our own time, the church added many false doctrines to the simple purity of the gospel—such as the notion that paying money to the church ("indulgences") could take the place of repentance for sin.

The Protestant Reformers challenged the corruption of the popes, who had become drunk with worldly power and greed. The Reformers demanded a return to the purity of God's Word and the simplicity of the gospel. As the church returned to the simple message of salvation from which it was born, the good news of Jesus Christ went out with renewed power—and the light of the gospel ended the Dark Ages. It has happened before and it can happen again.

But it must begin with you and me.

Western civilization was built on the Protestant Reformation. Yet our civilization has lost its moral and spiritual integrity and is coming apart at the seams. We have the Internet and iPhones and space probes exploring the solar system to Pluto and beyond. We can read God's exquisite creation, the human genome, like a road map—and we think we live in an age of enlightenment.

But all of this is a thin veneer of civilization hiding a dark and savage reality. Our culture has become hostile to God's Word and God's people. We have legalized abortion right up to the moment of birth. Our children can no longer expect privacy and safety in a school restroom or locker room. Our government promotes single parenthood and creates financial incentives for breaking up families. Our leaders place a hand on the Bible and swear to defend the Constitution, then proceed to violate it repeatedly while lining their own pockets. Our culture was founded on faith in God, yet all references to God and the Bible are being scrubbed from the public square.

We are living in the New Dark Ages. The only way the world can emerge from the New Dark Ages is the same way it emerged from the first Dark Ages—by returning to the purity of the gospel.

THE FALL OF ROME

The first Dark Ages began with the fall of Rome, symbolized by the sack of Rome by the Visigoths in AD 410. At the time, Rome—the so-called Eternal City—was the largest city in the world, with a population of eight hundred thousand, and it had not been conquered in eight hundred years. Alaric I, the king of the barbarian Visigoths, had been a commander in the Roman army. Denied a promotion to general, he led a rebellion, formed an army, and laid siege to Rome.

During the siege, panic reigned in the streets of Rome. Many wanted to return to the worship of the Roman gods, hoping that Jupiter, Mars, and the goddess Bellona might save them from the Visigoths. The historian Zosimus, in *Historia Nova*, recorded that Pope Innocent I agreed to permit sacrifices to the Roman gods, if the gods might defend Rome from the barbarians.[12] The church had sunk that low! It may have been the pope's appeasement of paganism that sealed the city's fate.

The Visigoth siege continued off and on for two years. Starvation and disease spread throughout the city. Thousands of slaves who had once propped up the Roman economy fled the city and joined the Visigoths. Finally, on August 24, 410, the Visigoths entered Rome through the Salarian Gate and pillaged the city for three days, raping and killing, and taking many citizens as slaves. The Visigoths were the terrorists of that time.

The Roman Empire was the superpower of that era. Rome had welcomed immigrants from all over the world, including the barbarian Visigoths. Rome was the epitome of power, culture, and civilization—*yet the empire collapsed before the people's eyes.*

WHATEVER GOES WRONG, BLAME THE CHRISTIANS

The sack of Rome left all Romans, both Christians and pagans, in a state of shock. Just as pagans today blame Christians for all the world's ills, the pagans of the Roman Empire blamed

Christians for the fall of Rome. In troubled times, Christians are often scapegoated.

In June 2016, after a Muslim man gunned down forty-nine people and wounded more than fifty others in a gay nightclub in Orlando, Florida, the news media rushed to judgment—and blamed *Christians*. Though the gunman claimed to be inspired by ISIS and an Islamist suicide bomber, the news media laid this attack at the doorstep of *Christians*. Why?

Because Christians had opposed same-sex marriage.

An American Civil Liberties Union attorney tweeted, "The Christian Right has introduced 200 anti-LGBT [Lesbian Gay Bisexual Transgender] bills in the last six months, and people are blaming Islam for this. No." And after former Arkansas governor Mike Huckabee expressed prayers for the victims, a lesbian novelist replied, "We don't want your hypocritical prayers. You led the fight against LGBT people. You promote this every day."[13]

An op-ed piece by the editorial board of the *New York Times* also blamed same-sex marriage opponents—Christians and conservatives—for the nightclub attack. The *Times* editors reasoned that the gunman "was driven by hatred toward gays and lesbians. Hate crimes don't happen in a vacuum. . . . [The victims] need to be remembered as casualties of a society where hate has deep roots."[14]

It is ISIS that throws gay men off of buildings and stones them in the streets,[15] yet the media blamed Christians. The gunman was radicalized in a Florida mosque, yet the media condemned the church. The Islamists are taking over Europe and infiltrating America, yet Christians get the blame. This has been the pattern ever since the sack of Rome: whatever goes wrong, blame the Christians.

The apostle Peter was deeply concerned that the church would distort the gospel with unbiblical additions. He warned against false teachers who would "secretly introduce destructive heresies, even denying the sovereign Lord who bought them—bringing swift destruction on themselves" (2 Peter 2:1). By the time of the fall of Rome, strange ideas, not found in Scripture, had crept into the church. For example, some church leaders taught that Mary, the mother of Jesus, plays a role in our salvation and redemption. They called Mary *Theotokos* ("Mother of God")—a title that was made official at the Council of Ephesus in 431. These early stirrings of the veneration of Mary eventually led to a whole host of Marian doctrines that treat her as a goddess to whom we should pray.

I honor Mary for her obedience to God in giving birth to the Lord Jesus Christ. But I believe the best honor we can pay her is to remember that it is Jesus, not Mary, to whom all glory, honor, and prayers are rightfully due.

The Christians of Rome in AD 410 were confident that God would never take His hand of protection from Rome. At that time, the people of Rome considered the Roman Empire a Christian nation. They were astonished when the barbarians stormed into the city, plundering and pillaging, just as the ancient Israelites were shocked when the Babylonians stormed into Jerusalem and conquered the nation.

Most Americans have the same confidence that America is invincible and that God will never remove His hand of blessing and protection. But there are no guarantees that America could not fall just as Israel and Rome fell. The forces of political Islam plan to raise the black flag of conquest over our land. Not only do we have no plans for preventing our downfall, but we seem bent on reliving the most horrifying lessons of the past.

4

THE CITY OF MAN AND THE CITY OF GOD

THE FALL OF ROME left the Christians of the Roman Empire feeling disillusioned and devastated. During this time of great suffering and confusion, God raised up a man from North Africa named Augustine (354–430). His Latin name was Aurelius Augustinus Hipponensis. Augustine disliked the name Aurelius because it was the name of a Roman emperor, Marcus Aurelius. So he chose to be known as Augustinus Hipponensis—Augustine of Hippo.

During Augustine's early years, his mother, Monica, had one passion in her heart: that her beloved son would follow Jesus as his Lord and Savior. She prayed for him day after day—and she is an example to all of us godly parents and grandparents: don't ever give up praying for your children and grandchildren, no matter how far they have strayed.

Augustine was in North Africa in AD 354 and spent his early years in Milan, Italy. There he lived a wild and hedonistic life. Yet God abundantly answered Monica's prayers for her wayward son. Augustine experienced a dramatic conversion in 386, at the age of thirty-one. His mother had prayed fervently for him for more than three decades.

Around the year 400, fourteen years after his conversion, Augustine wrote and published his *Confessions*—his Christian testimony. In the thirteen chapters of that book, he explained how the grace of the Lord Jesus Christ, through faith alone, could save and redeem sinners like himself. On the first page of his *Confessions*, Augustine addressed God, saying, "You have formed us for yourself, and our hearts are restless until they find rest in you."[1]

After his conversion to Christ, Augustine was baptized and placed himself under the tutelage of Ambrose, the godly bishop of Milan. Augustine delved deeply into the Scriptures—and there he discovered a profound truth: salvation is by grace through faith alone. That, of course, is the same world-changing insight that, more than a thousand years later, would transform the thinking of a monk named Martin Luther, who would become one of the founders of the Protestant Reformation.

In 388, Augustine moved to Hippo Regius (where the

city of Annaba, Algeria, stands today), and in 395, he was made bishop of that city. There he became a famous preacher, striving against the false doctrines of the Manichaean cult.

Then, in 410, news of the sack of Rome came to Augustine. Just as the Babylonian captivity led the people of Israel to rediscover the Word of God, and just as the abuses and injustices of the Dark Ages would later lead the Reformers to rediscover the Word of God, so the fall of Rome led Augustine to a rediscovery and reaffirmation of the authority of God's Word.

Augustine saw the suffering and bewilderment of the Christian community in Rome. He wanted to console and encourage the believers, and refute the claim that the sack of Rome was the revenge of the pagan gods against the Christianized Roman Empire. So he picked up his pen again and began writing.

TWO CITIES

In his book *The City of God*, Augustine argued that there are two cities in opposition to each other—the heavenly City of God and the earthly City of Man. Augustine wanted believers to know that the City of God would ultimately triumph.

The City of God, he said, is made up of all those who love God and want to serve Him faithfully. It is made up of all people who dedicate themselves to living out the eternal truths of God's Word. The City of Man, by contrast, consists of those who chase the pleasures and priorities of this dying world.

These two cities are at war with each other. They come from different origins. They are progressing along separate paths. They have radically different destinies.

But here is an all-important truth about these two cities that we must clearly understand: We who are citizens of the City of God must, at least for now, live as sojourners in the City of Man. We are *of* the City of God, yet we are *in* the City of Man.

Augustine wrote *The City of God* to help us understand how we ought to live as God's people in the City of Man. We must live in the City of Man without being tainted by its philosophies or stained by its sins. We must not only *survive* in the City of Man, but we must *thrive* here, so that we can proclaim the good news and attract people to the City of God.

One of the great illusions the City of Man clings to is that the City of Man can become the City of God. There is a mind-set in the City of Man that says human beings are perfectible through education, through indoctrination, through political initiatives and social programs. This view holds that if we provide the right cultural environment, we can perfect the human race and bring about a utopia—a humanly designed, completely secular "City of God."

But the City of Man can never become the City of God. The human race is not perfectible by education or politics or social engineering. The human race, though created in the image of God, has been broken and bent by sin. There is no human agency that can repair or perfect humanity.

Only the good news of Jesus Christ can move a human being from bondage in the City of Man to salvation in the City of God.

THE BOOKENDS OF THE BIBLE

When you read through the Bible from Genesis to Revelation, you are struck by its consistency. There are certain themes that echo and re-echo down through its pages, from the Old Testament to the New.

The Bible begins with a wedding in the City of God, in a paradise called the Garden of Eden. In that wedding, God joins together a man and woman, and the man says, "This is now bone of my bones and flesh of my flesh; she shall be called 'woman,' for she was taken out of man." And the Bible adds, "That is why a man leaves his father and mother and is united to his wife, and they become one flesh" (Genesis 2:23–24).

And how does the Bible end? With a wedding in the City of God, in a paradise called the New Jerusalem. It is the wedding supper of the Lamb, a symbolic wedding between the Bridegroom, Jesus, and His bride, the church (Revelation 19:6–9).

The Bible begins with Adam and Eve as vice-regents—

rulers over creation under the authority of God the Creator. The Bible ends with the redeemed saints reigning as vice-regents with Jesus in the new creation. The Bible begins with a scene of peace, tranquillity, and joy in the City of God, and it ends with even greater peace, tranquillity, and joy in the City of God.

Between the beginning and the end of the Bible, we see story after story of men and women who are citizens of the City of God, yet they live faithfully and fruitfully in the City of Man. The Bible is God's revelation of Himself to the world—a world that hates God and rebels against His plan. That's why the systems and leaders of this world want to remove God's Word from the public square, from our schools, and from our media.

The Bible begins with the City of God (Eden) and ends with the City of God (the New Jerusalem). But between the beginning and the end is the story of the city where we now live—the City of Man. And that city is a battlefield.

IN THE CITY OF MAN, BUT NOT *OF* IT

As Christians, we are not *of* the City of Man, but we are *in* it. We are engaged in a good fight against our implacable enemy, Satan. We struggle against the corrupting influence of the world. We struggle against the temptations of our own flesh. This struggle will not end until we reach our eternal home, the City of God.

Like Eve, we often question God's intentions and His Word. We say, "We're not sure what God really said. We're not sure what God really meant. We're not sure if what He said is relevant for us today." Some even say, "We know what God said, but we can't help our urges. We choose to live according to our feelings and desires, not God's commandments." Our disobedience produces the inevitable consequences: God must cast us out of the City of God and hand us over to the City of Man. He must send us into exile, in order to bring us back to our senses and call us to repentance.

The first City of God, the Garden of Eden, was created by God in perfection and beauty. It provided everything human beings needed for a utopian life, including delightful food and secure protection. Yet Adam and Eve found themselves evicted from Eden, cast out into the City of Man, because they wanted independence from God. They did not want to submit to God's loving, sheltering authority.

This tragedy has played out countless times throughout human history. God provided for His people in the City of God—but they chose self-will over God's will and were cast out into the cold and cruel City of Man. After their expulsion from the City of God, they lived lives of suffering, sorrow, and regret. In our fallenness and willfulness, we repeatedly choose the reeking, smoldering garbage dump of the City of Man over the beauty and splendor of the City of God.

We know the consequences of sin, yet we glare at God in

defiance and bite down on the forbidden fruit. The Bible tells us that the pleasures of sin are fleeting (Hebrews 11:25). We know it's true. Yet we willingly choose the fleeting pleasures of sin, fully aware that the consequences of our sin may haunt us for a lifetime.

I have talked to a number of high school graduates who told me they couldn't wait to get away from home and be out on their own. There's nothing wrong with that. It's normal and healthy for young people to seek the independence of adulthood. But many of these same young people, when they confront a major problem in life, can't wait to hurry home, back to the safe and secure arms of Mom and Dad.

There is an analogy here to the human being who seeks to be independent from God. We may think it's great fun to ignore God and His law, to indulge every selfish desire, to live as if there were no consequences. Then one day, disaster strikes—and we cry out to God, "Lord, rescue me! Make me safe and secure once more!"

God will always love us, accept us, forgive us, and restore us—but He won't always erase the consequences of our sinful choices. When we refuse to live by God's law, when we choose to live by our own selfish desires, we move ourselves outside the protective walls of the City of God—and we take up residence in the dangerous slums of the City of Man.

Sin is pleasurable for a moment—but a moment of drunkenness can leave you paralyzed for life. Sin is pleasurable for a moment—but a moment of getting high may condemn you to a lifelong addiction. Sin is pleasurable for a moment—but a moment of sexual indulgence could destroy your marriage or give you AIDS. Sin is pleasurable for a moment—but a moment of pleasure could end your life and condemn you to eternal destruction.

The first City of God, the Garden of Eden, was a paradise of God's endless provision. God gave Adam and Eve purposeful work to do. They tended the garden that produced the food they ate. The people of the City of God view their work differently from the rest of humanity, as Paul explains: "Whatever you do, work at it with all your heart. . . . It is the Lord Christ you are serving" (Colossians 3:23–24).

Unbelievers tend to resent their work. That's why many of them are clock watchers and goof-offs. That's why some of them steal from their employers and pad their expense accounts. A lazy, dishonest worker is fit only for the City of Man. Such people have a sense of entitlement and no sense of responsibility.

When you work for the glory of God, you can't wait to go to work. You don't see work as drudgery. It's a privilege and a ministry. All day long, your work brings you face-to-face with people who live in quiet desperation in the City of Man. You can display to them the joy of knowing Jesus. The light of the Lord Jesus can shine through your life, even when you are not witnessing with words.

Even if your job involves picking up trash or crawling under buildings or performing some other unpleasant task, you can honor God with your labor. You can bless others with your attitude of joy. You can know that your work is purposeful and meaningful, because you touch many lives throughout your workday.

Honest work creates wealth and blessing for you, your family, and your society. So the work you perform is much like the work Adam and Eve performed in the first City of God. You can take pleasure and pride in your work, knowing that God takes pleasure and pride in you.

When Adam and Eve were in harmony with God, they were in harmony with each other. When they were in harmony with God, they were in harmony with their environment. That's what made the Garden of Eden a paradise.

What was true of Adam and Eve is true in my own life. When I am not in harmony with God, when I have unconfessed sin in my life, I am not in harmony with myself or others. No matter where I physically live, when I am in harmony with God, I'm in paradise—I'm in the City of God. I experience God's provision and protection.

The Bible describes the coming City of God, the New Jerusalem, as a city enclosed by walls of protection. The first City of God sheltered Adam and Eve in much the same way. God provided for Adam and Eve and protected them in the Garden. When they chose rebellion and self-will, they removed themselves from the protective walls of the City of God. They made themselves vulnerable to danger and death.

When you live according to God's will and God's Word, you are surrounded by the City of God wherever you go. You may be *in* the City of Man, but you are not *of* the City of Man. You are *of* the City of God.

TRUE SAFETY

I have traveled to places that are considered dangerous, places where there is political unrest or crime or terrorist activity. While I was preparing to depart, my beloved brothers and sisters in Christ have said to me, "Oh, Pastor, are you sure you should go? Please be careful. Stay safe. Don't take any chances. We will be praying day and night for your safety."

I appreciate the loving concern of these brothers and sisters more than I can say. But let me tell you something: I am safer in the middle of a battlefield when I'm in the will of God than I am in my own bedroom when I'm outside the will of God.

The same is true for every believer. If it's safety and protection you want, make sure you are walking in the will of God. Make sure the City of God surrounds you wherever you go.

Over the years, many people have asked a good question: Why did God plant the tree of the knowledge of good and evil in that perfect place? Why was that tree planted in the

Garden of Eden, where Satan might use it as an object of temptation?

I can answer that question: The tree was there to remind Adam and Eve that they were not their own. It was there to remind them that they were God's own possession. The tree was there to remind them that they were accountable to God and that they could not escape judgment for the moral choices they made.

The tree was not placed there by accident. God deliberately placed that tree in the Garden of Eden. And there in that Garden, the first man, Adam, met temptation—and he was defeated by sin.

But thousands of years later, there was another garden—the Garden of Gethsemane. In the Garden of Eden, Adam fell and we all fell with him (Romans 5:12). In the Garden of Gethsemane, Jesus was victorious, and all who belong to Him are victorious as well. In the Garden of Eden, the disobedience of one man caused sin to infect all of humanity. But in the Garden of Gethsemane, the obedience of one Man produced the antidote for sin.

In the Garden of Eden, Adam experienced death as a consequence of his rebellion. But in the Garden of Gethsemane, we all experience life—eternal life—by grace through faith. One tree in Eden defeated Adam, and another tree, the cross of Christ, defeated sin and Satan. One tree brought the knowledge of evil, but the other tree gave us power over evil, power over temptation, power over death, the power of salvation.

So the question is, which tree do you look to? The tree by which humanity was tempted and fell? Or the tree by which God gave us eternal life? Do you belong to the City of God—or to the City of Man?

WHICH CITY WILL YOU CHOOSE?

From biblical times to the present day, we have always had a choice between two competing ways of life, two civilizations: the City of God or the City of Man. One choice leads to blessing; the other brings a curse. Those who make the rebellious and self-destructive choice will reap the harvest of that choice.

Adam and Eve chose—and they were exiled from the Garden of Eden. The nation of Israel chose—and the people were exiled from the land of promise. We in the church today are making our choice. What harvest will we reap?

The door of repentance, the door of blessing, still stands open—at least for a while. The church can still return to the purity of God's truth. And if the church would be faithful to the Word of God, if we would stop adulterating His Word with the philosophies and false religions of this dying culture, we might yet see the rise of a New Reformation instead of a descent into another Dark Age.

For now, we all must live in the City of Man—but we

don't have to belong to it. Our citizenship, if we know Jesus as Lord and Savior, is in the City of God. Only the cross of Jesus Christ, who shed His blood for us, can bring us a life of purpose. Only the cross of Jesus Christ can give us hope in a world of hopelessness, light in a world of darkness, joy in a world of sorrow, peace in a world of turmoil, and confidence in a world of terror.

That is why we must choose to belong to the City of God. That is why we must choose to follow God and live according to His will. We can walk the dark and dangerous streets of the City of Man with our heads held high. If we belong to Jesus and He is our security, we do not fear the threats of the barbarians.

We are citizens of the City of God.

5

CHOICES THAT CHANGE HISTORY

TWENTY-SIX-YEAR-OLD BLOGGER Claire Eastham is beautiful, funny, and intelligent. She had a happy childhood, enjoys a fulfilling relationship with her boyfriend, and works at what she describes as her "dream job" at a well-known book publishing house. Yet, not long ago, the panic attacks Claire has suffered since she was a teenager started to dominate her life. These attacks became so intense that she had to take a monthlong leave of absence from work. She says, "Panic attacks are the worst. You feel like you're going mad, like you're going to die; worrying about everything, feeling out of control, wondering what you sound like and what you look like. The voice in your head, it's constant. You can't stop it. It's exhausting."[1]

In May 2016, the *Guardian* (UK), one of the world's most respected newspapers, published a story about the growing sense of fear, restlessness, and anxiety around the world. The newspaper reported:

> We live with an epidemic of anxiety. In 1980, 4 percent of Americans suffered a mental disorder associated with anxiety. Today half do. . . . Anxiety, depression, self-harm, attention deficit disorder and profound eating problems afflict our young as never before.
>
> Anxiety has always been part of the human condition—as has depression and tendencies to self-harm—but never, it seems, on this scale. A number of trends appear to be colliding. . . . The bonds of society, faith and community—tried and tested mechanisms to support wellbeing—are fraying. Teenagers . . . are beset by a myriad of agonizing choices about how to achieve the good life with fewer social and psychological anchors to help them navigate their way. Who can blame them if they respond with an ever rising sense of anxiety, if not panic?[2]

What is the cause of this growing global state of anxiety and fear? The *Guardian* attributes this disturbing trend to a "fraying" or breakdown of "the bonds of society, faith and community." In other words, the defection of the church from its foundation of faith, with a resulting collapse of the family, social norms, and the cohesion of community, has left people feeling vulnerable, fearful, and depressed. By defecting from God's Word, we in the church have let society down.

The Israelites, in the time of their defection before they were conquered by the Babylonians, experienced the same sense of fear and vulnerability that people in Western civilization feel today. Government became impotent. The laws were flouted and ignored. Violence and strife were rampant throughout society. Evil went unpunished.

The prophet Habakkuk expressed the mood of his times when he poured out his complaint to God:

> How long, LORD, must I call for help,
>   but you do not listen?
> Or cry out to you, "Violence!"
>   but you do not save?
> Why do you make me look at injustice?
>   Why do you tolerate wrongdoing?
> Destruction and violence are before me;
>   there is strife, and conflict abounds.
> Therefore the law is paralyzed,
>   and justice never prevails.
> The wicked hem in the righteous,
>   so that justice is perverted. (Habakkuk 1:2–4)

Though little is known about the prophet Habakkuk, Bible scholars believe he lived in Jerusalem at about the same time as the prophets Jeremiah and Zephaniah. After the people of Israel had spent two centuries in disobedience and rebellion, Habakkuk delivered a series of prophecies from God concerning the Babylonian Empire. Through him, God said:

> I am raising up the Babylonians,
>   that ruthless and impetuous people,
> who sweep across the whole earth
>   to seize dwellings not their own.
> They are a feared and dreaded people;
>   they are a law to themselves
>   and promote their own honor. (Habakkuk 1:6–7)

There are always consequences when God's people cease to honor God and obey His Word. When the Israelites turned their backs on God, He removed His hand of protection from them. They became victims of the terrorists of their day, the Babylonians. Read Habakkuk's description of the Babylonians—"ruthless and impetuous people, who sweep across the whole earth . . . a feared and dreaded people . . . a law to themselves." Isn't that an apt description of terror groups such as ISIS?

If we, as God's people, distort God's truth in order to line our pockets or to become friends with the world, don't we risk the same consequences Habakkuk warned about here?

TERROR FROM WITHOUT, SOCIAL DECAY FROM WITHIN

Exile is the destiny of every society or community that once knew God, then turned its back on Him. That exile might take any of a number of forms, but it almost always includes terror from without and social decay from within. Examples of that social decay include the following:

1. *Eroding respect for truth and wisdom.* Our Western universities are no longer institutions of higher learning but brainwashing factories. Students are not trained to be wise and learned but are simply indoctrinated into the party line. Graduates have very little knowledge of the classics, the humanities, economics, or history. They cannot find the nations of the world on a map. They know just enough to be easily manipulated by secularist propaganda.

2. *Declining respect for integrity in our leaders.* Americans used to demand character and virtue from their leaders. From Watergate to the Monica Lewinsky scandal to the still-unexplained massacre at Benghazi, it's clear that Americans have not always gotten the honest government they voted for—but at least the voters used to care about the integrity of our country's leaders. Not anymore! Today, American voters

elect the demagogue who promises the most freebies, not the leader with proven character.

3. *Increasing corruption in government.* Our leaders no longer answer to We the People but to a wealthy clique of oligarchs. Legislators write laws that benefit the powerful few so that billion-dollar corporations reap government subsidies while the middle class is crushed by oppressive taxation. The welfare state subsidizes indolence and irresponsible parenting while punishing hard work and achievement.

4. *An upsurge of violence and race hatred.* Our media and politicians stir up racial hatred and division for the sake of ratings and political advantage. We are emptying our prisons and turning predators loose, placing innocent citizens—especially our minority populations—at ever-increasing risk.

5. *The coarsening of the culture.* Vulgarity and obscenity are rampant, not merely in the darkest corners of the Internet but throughout our entire society. The debasement of our Western civilization is another sign of our Babylonian Exile.

6. *Economic instability and institutionalized greed.* Our politicians do nothing to solve the national debt. Left unchecked, the debt will reach critical mass and collapse the world economy. The chaos that will erupt when the crash occurs will be like nothing the world has ever seen before. The coming crash is 100 percent preventable, but it continues to worsen because of insatiable human greed.

All of these internal threats, combined with the external

threat of terrorism, are signs of our Babylonian Exile. These problems *can* be solved—and you and I are the solution. If we would return to the truth of God's Word, if we would become the light of the world as the Lord called us to be (Matthew 5:14–16), then the light of God's truth, shining through us, would push back the darkness.

The apostle Paul tells us that God has called us to be "blameless and pure," living as "children of God without fault in a warped and crooked generation." If we would live blameless lives, exemplifying the purity and simplicity of the gospel, then we would "shine among them like stars in the sky" (Philippians 2:15). Wouldn't you like to shine like a star in the firmament of this dark and dying world? Wouldn't you like to shed the light of Jesus Christ on the hopeless people around you?

If we would answer that call and take up that challenge, then we would see more and more people come to know Christ—and God would heal our land (2 Chronicles 7:14). Our exile into terrorism would come to an end.

PEACE IN AN ANXIOUS WORLD

Restlessness, worry, and anxiety continue to grow around the world, and I believe this is a preparation for the coming of the Antichrist. We don't know God's timetable for the Last Days. We don't know if the events of the book of Revelation will be set in motion today or ten thousand years from now.

Jesus doesn't want us to speculate on the day or the hour of His return (Matthew 24:36; 25:13). He simply wants us to be ready at all times.

Yet I can't help feeling that the Last Days are fast approaching. Our restlessness and anxiety began when humanity was evicted from the first City of God, the Garden of Eden. But the fear that seized human hearts after the fall of mankind seems to be growing exponentially, spiraling out of control.

If there is one feature that separates the citizens of the City of God from dwellers of the City of Man, it is anxiety. Those who belong to the City of God have nothing to fear. Those who belong to the City of Man have everything to fear. This doesn't mean that God's people never experience anxiety or fear. We all do from time to time. But we who live in the City of God have a Source of hope, peace, and confidence that those in the City of Man don't have. As the apostle Paul assured us, "And the peace of God, which transcends all understanding, will guard your hearts and your minds in Christ Jesus" (Philippians 4:7).

That's why Jesus repeatedly told His followers, "Do not worry":

Do not worry about your life, what you will eat or drink; or about your body, what you will wear. Is not life more than food, and the body more than clothes?

Look at the birds of the air; they do not sow or reap or store away in barns, and yet your heavenly Father feeds them. Are you not much more valuable than they? (Matthew 6:25–26)

Do not worry about tomorrow, for tomorrow will worry about itself. (Matthew 6:34)

Do not worry about what to say or how to say it. At that time you will be given what to say, for it will not be you speaking, but the Spirit of your Father speaking through you. (Matthew 10:19–20)

Fear, worry, and anxiety overshadow the City of Man. But there should be no shadow of fear in the City of God.

In the midst of the gathering darkness and deepening depression of this world, is it possible to live without fear, worry, and anxiety? Yes! Absolutely! Those of us who belong to the City of God, who have placed our trust in the Lord Jesus, exemplify the peace of God in the midst of an anxious world.

TWO HUMANITIES

We can trace the contrast between the City of Man and the City of God throughout the Bible. These two cities came from two distinct origins, followed two different paths through history, display two distinct sets of characteristics, and are bound for two completely opposite destinations. The earthly city, the City of Man, is symbolized in Scripture as Egypt, as Babylon, as Rome. Our civilization, Western civilization, is the City of Man today.

By contrast, the heavenly city, the City of God, is a symbol of all the elect of God from every nation, every tribe, every generation. All the redeemed followers of the Lord, from Old Testament times and New Testament times, will one day dwell in the New Jerusalem—the true City of God. When the City of God arrives, the City of Man will be destroyed. But the City of God will go on forever and ever.

These two cities represent two distinct humanities—two distinct offspring, or lineages. One is the lineage of Satan; the other is the lineage of Eve.

We first see this distinction in Genesis 3:15, immediately after the fall of Adam and Eve. There we find the first announcement of the gospel. There, in the Garden of Eden, God tells the serpent, Satan, "I will put enmity between you and the woman, and between your offspring and hers; he will crush your head, and you will strike his heel."

Now, in a biological and genetic sense, all of Eve's offspring are a single lineage—the human race. But God is not speaking in a biological sense. He is speaking of spiritual reality. The offspring of Satan consists of all fallen, unregenerate human beings—those who have rejected God and have rejected His Son as their Lord and Savior. The offspring of Eve—her ultimate descendant—is the Lord Jesus Christ.

God's prophecy, spoken to Satan in the Garden of Eden, was fulfilled on the cross of Calvary. There Satan struck at the heel of Jesus, the offspring of Eve. His head was pierced by a crown of thorns, the bones of His hands and feet were dislocated by massive iron nails, and His side was gashed by a Roman spear. Yet compared to what Jesus accomplished on the cross—crushing the head of Satan—all of the Lord's sufferings were like a snakebite on the heel.

Jesus suffered, died, and rose again—but Satan will never recover from the skull-crushing blow he received on that day.

We see another description of the enmity between the offspring of Satan and the offspring of Eve in the book of Revelation:

> A great sign appeared in heaven: a woman clothed with the sun, with the moon under her feet and a crown of twelve stars on her head. She was pregnant and cried out in pain as she was about to give birth. Then another sign appeared in heaven: an enormous red dragon with seven heads and ten horns and seven crowns on its heads. Its tail swept a third of the stars out of the sky and flung them to the earth. The dragon stood in front of the woman who was about to give birth, so that it might devour her child

the moment he was born. She gave birth to a son, a male child, who "will rule all the nations with an iron scepter." And her child was snatched up to God and to his throne. The woman fled into the wilderness to a place prepared for her by God, where she might be taken care of for 1,260 days. (Revelation 12:1–6)

Here again, we see the woman and her offspring contrasted with Satan—"the dragon"—who seeks to devour the woman's offspring. We even see the dragon in his act of rebellion against God, leading a third of the angels of heaven against God, resulting in Satan being exiled from God's presence.

Sin created the enmity between the offspring of Satan and the offspring of Eve. Sin created the distinction between the City of Man and the City of God. Disobedience to God always brings division.

When the serpent—Satan—tempted Adam and Eve, he had two goals in mind. First, Satan wanted to stop Adam and Eve from worshipping God. Second, Satan wanted to seduce Adam and Eve into worshipping him. Satan succeeded in his first objective, but not in the second. He succeeded in destroying the fellowship Adam and Eve enjoyed with God, but he did not seduce them into worshipping him.

Why did Satan fail in his second objective? He might have succeeded except for one obstacle in Satan's way: the gospel of Jesus Christ. When God announced the gospel in Genesis 3:15, when he pronounced Satan's ultimate doom, he also announced to Adam and Eve that a Savior was coming. He announced a solution to the problem of sin.

Adam and Eve were the first human beings to be created, the first to sin—and the first to hear the gospel of Jesus Christ. They heard the gospel, and they believed. That is why Satan could not seduce them into worshipping him.

Why did Satan want Adam and Eve to worship him? Was it because Satan thought so highly of these human creatures God had created? Was he so impressed with us that he craved fellowship with us? Absolutely not. Satan hated Adam and Eve from the moment they were created. Satan's heart burned with jealousy toward God's newest creation, the human race.

Why was Satan jealous? He was jealous because he had once been the most beautiful and splendid creature of God's creation. The book of Ezekiel gives us God's description of Satan before his rebellion and fall. There, God reminds Satan:

> You were the seal of perfection,
>   full of wisdom and perfect in beauty.
> You were in Eden,
>   the garden of God;
> every precious stone adorned you. . . .
> Your settings and mountings were made of gold;
>   on the day you were created they were prepared.

You were anointed as a guardian cherub,
    for so I ordained you.
You were on the holy mount of God;
    you walked among the fiery stones.
You were blameless in your ways
    from the day you were created
    till wickedness was found in you. (Ezekiel 28:12–15)

Satan was created as a creature of dazzling beauty, knowledge, and wisdom. But the sin of pride entered Satan's heart, and he rebelled against God. As a result, Satan was cast out of heaven. When Satan saw God create human beings in God's own image and place them in the Garden of Eden, he was filled with rage and envy. God showered these creatures with love and placed them in a beautiful garden and graced them with His fellowship. Satan had lost all of this—his beauty, his special relationship with God, and his place in paradise. Satan was determined to make sure that the human creatures could not have what he himself had lost.

So he pretended to be Eve's friend, even as he was tempting her to destruction. Satan thought he could lure Adam and Eve away from obeying and worshipping God (and he was right). But he also thought he could switch their allegiance and persuade them to worship him instead.

Satan didn't understand the power of the gospel to alter our attitude toward sin and draw us into worship of the one true God. The Bible says that when the gospel transforms a person's heart, "the new creation has come: the old has gone, the new is here!" (2 Corinthians 5:17). The Lord Jesus Christ alone has the power to rescue us from Satan's darkness and bring us into His kingdom of light—"the kingdom of the Son he loves, in whom we have redemption, the forgiveness of sins" (Colossians 1:13–14).

We are no longer citizens of the fallen and dying City of Man. The gospel has granted us *eternal citizenship* in the City of God.

6

A DIVIDING WALL OF ENMITY

BEFORE CHRIST came into my life, I liked sin. I was raised in a Christian home in Egypt, and my seven brothers and sisters were all faithful and well-behaved. I was the rebellious one, and I continually broke my mother's heart with my waywardness.

My mother was always in poor health, and she nearly died giving birth to me. Her doctors had urged her to consent to a therapeutic abortion, but my mother refused to abort me, even to save her own life. When I was born, she dedicated me to serving God and named me Michael—"messenger of God"—as a symbol of the life she hoped and prayed I would lead.

My mother lived for years in anguish and disappointment

THE BARBARIANS ARE HERE

over my disobedience. It seemed that all her prayers for my future as a "messenger of God" went unanswered. The grief and frustration I selfishly inflicted on my mother took a toll on her health.

One day, when I was fifteen, my mother took me aside and warned me that my rebelliousness would destroy my life. I smirked and dismissed her warning.

"Michael," she said, "you don't listen to what I say!"

"I'm listening," I said, waiting for her to stop talking so I could go out with my friends.

"No, Michael," she said, "you hear my words but you don't listen!"

She was right—but I didn't care. I felt no remorse because *I liked sin.* And I had no intention of changing the way I lived my life.

My mother could see the defiance in my eyes, so in desperation she placed her hand on my head and began to pray. "Lord," she said, "I have always believed and prayed that Michael would be the one who would serve You with all his heart. But if I've been wrong, if Michael is not going to serve You, then I pray You would take him now."

Those words shocked me more than anything my mother had ever said. She had risked her life to give birth to me—yet she was inviting God to slay me if I refused to serve Him. That was the first time I realized how deeply I had hurt my mother with my disobedience.

Did her prayer change my ways? No—I remained selfish and rebellious. But her prayer haunted me. I couldn't grasp the contradiction: my mother loved me with all her heart, yet she would rather see me dead than living in disobedience to God.

A few months after my mother prayed that desperate prayer over me, I went to my brother Samir and asked him for help with my math studies. Samir, who would eventually become a finance official in the Egyptian government, agreed to tutor me in math—*if* I would go with him to an evangelistic meeting.

I was desperate for his help, so I agreed to go—but I planned to sit and mock everything the evangelist said. During the service, however, I found myself unable to mock his message. The evangelist preached from Hosea and talked about how God is patient with wayward children—but one day, God's patience will run out. The Day of Judgment is coming, and the door of God's patience will shut forever.

I felt God calling me to repent, because I might never have another opportunity. So, on the evening of March 4, 1964, at the age of sixteen, I rose up and was the first to respond to the evangelist's invitation. I gave my life to Jesus Christ, and my life was changed forever. I'm so glad I made that decision when I did.

The same night I made that decision, my mother went into the hospital. I wrote her a letter, telling her about the decision I had made to serve the Lord. She kept that letter under her pillow, and whenever anyone visited her in the hospital, she proudly showed them the letter. "Now," she said, "I can die in peace."

Four months after I committed my life to Christ, my mother passed away. I'm so glad she died knowing her prayers for me had been answered.

Ever since I made that commitment, there has been a difference in the way I look at sin. Before my conversion, I enjoyed sin. I didn't want to suffer the consequences of sin, but I liked continuing in sin. After my conversion, I hated sin. The presence of God in my life made sin a miserable experience. I still sinned, but not as frequently, and I could no longer enjoy it. Sin left me feeling guilty and ashamed. When I sinned, I felt I was betraying Christ and letting Him down—because I was.

Why did my conversion experience create such a different attitude toward sin? It's because God has placed enmity between the woman and the serpent, between Eve's offspring (Jesus) and Satan's offspring (unregenerate sinners). There is a dividing wall of enmity between me (a child of Jesus) and Satan. Because I love Jesus, I hate sin. I can testify personally that the gospel has the power to alter the way we feel about sin.

Because of the wall of enmity that exists between Christians and Satan, we should not be surprised when

Christians are hated and attacked by the offspring of Satan. We should not be shocked when we are mocked and maligned and marginalized. We should not think it strange when they not only verbally attack us but also seek to do us harm, destroy our reputations, destroy us professionally and financially, and even—like the Islamist barbarians—try to kill us.

There are two distinct humanities—the spiritual descendants of the serpent and the spiritual descendants of the woman. The spiritual descendants of the serpent are all those who obey the will of Satan, such as the barbarian terrorists and those who oppose or deny the Christian gospel. Whether they realize they are obeying Satan or not, whether they believe in the existence of Satan or not, they are doing Satan's bidding. Everyone who does the will of Satan is a spiritual descendant of the serpent.

THE CONTRAST OF CAIN AND ABEL

The enmity between these two humanities carries forward into Genesis 4 and 5. There we see clear evidence that Adam and Eve received the gospel that God gave in Genesis 3:15. They believed God's promise that He would send a Savior, the offspring of the woman. What is the evidence?

Genesis 4:1 tells us, "Adam made love to his wife Eve, and she became pregnant and gave birth to Cain. She said, 'With the help of the LORD I have brought forth a man.'"

The name of Eve's firstborn, Cain, literally means "possession."[1] In other words, when Eve gave birth and named her son Cain, she was saying, in effect, "I have brought forth a man. I now *possess* the man of the Lord's promise. God prophesied that I would bring forth an offspring who would crush the head of the serpent—and here he is!"

In this hope Eve would be disappointed, because Cain would later slay his brother Abel. Cain was not the offspring God had promised. The coming of the promised Messiah would not occur for thousands of years, long after Eve's physical death.

In fact, the story of Cain and his brother Abel serves as an object lesson in the contrast between these two humanities, the people of the City of Man and the people of the City of God. The story of Cain and Abel illustrates the enmity between these two humanities. Cain followed the will of Satan. Abel followed the will of God. Cain offered a sacrifice to God in a sinful and self-willed spirit—and God rejected his offering.

God had shown Adam and Eve the kind of sacrifice that was acceptable. God had killed a lamb and covered their nakedness with the lamb's skin. He taught them that without the shedding of blood, there could be no forgiveness of sin (Hebrews 9:22). He was showing them how He would solve the sin problem by shedding the blood of the innocent Lamb of God.

Cain's attitude was: "I know what God said, and I know what God wants—but I want to come to God *my* way. I'm going to bring God some grain. Instead of following the precepts God gave my parents, I will make up my own religion and offer a sacrifice in my own way." Thus the disobedience began.

A GOD WHO REASONS WITH US

God did not turn His back on Cain. Instead, He reasoned with Cain. He wanted Cain to repent of his sin and to return to the City of God. But Cain, in his anger and rebellion, killed his brother Abel, whose sacrifice was acceptable to God.

Even after Cain murdered his brother, God tried to reason with Cain and would have received him if he had returned to Him in true repentance. Cain chose his own fate. He chose to reject God and to reject the atonement God offered.

Here is a facet of God's character we easily miss: Our God reasons with us. He continually tries to reason with nonbelievers, with those who belong to the City of Man. "Come now, let us reason together, says the LORD: though your sins are like scarlet, they shall be as white as snow; though they are red like crimson, they shall become like wool," says God in Isaiah 1:18 (ESV).

This is a lesson for all of us who belong to the City of

God while living in the City of Man. I see many Christians wringing their hands and saying, "The world is getting so dark and dangerous. Our society has turned against us. We never dreamed we would see Christians so hated and mocked in our lifetime. The world is out of control. There's nothing to do but hide in the mountains and wait for the Lord to return."

No! That is not a godly response. We cannot simply write off humanity and walk away. Like God Himself, we must reason with those who belong to the City of Man. We must show them the light of Christ in the midst of their darkness. We must be salt, creating a thirst for God among them. As Jesus indicated, we are in the world but not of the world (John 17:14). So while we are in the world, let's keep living for Christ, speaking for Christ, and seeking to win the world for Christ.

We don't know which ones of the people around us are appointed unto salvation (1 Thessalonians 5:9). If we continue living godly lives and sharing the good news with others, some will join us. They will move from the City of Man to the City of God. We bring a fragrance of Christ into the City of Man, and we stir up a hunger among the dwellers of that city for the good news of Jesus Christ. Some will mock us, but some will believe.

The enmity between the City of God and the City of Man is etched into the story of Cain. After Cain killed his brother and lied to God, he was possessed by fear. He went out and built a city (Genesis 4:17)—the epitome of the City of Man. It was a city filled with fear and restlessness.

Cain, a fugitive from God, built the first City of Man as a place to escape to. He went there to hide from God. There he thought he could safely pretend that God didn't exist. In his guilt-ridden, anxious state, Cain complained to God, "I will be a restless wanderer on the earth, and whoever finds me will kill me" (Genesis 4:14).

Like so many people around us, Cain had just enough of a conscience to be tormented by fear, but not enough conscience to turn to God.

AMBASSADORS FOR THE CITY OF GOD

The leaders of our society today are still trying to build the perfect City of Man—a city in which all Christian influence has been eradicated from the public square. We saw such an attempt in Houston, Texas, in 2014. When the city council and the mayor passed the Houston Equal Rights Ordinance, or HERO, they said that their objective was to end discrimination against citizens based on a number of factors, including gender identity.

Opponents of the ordinance, especially conservative Christians, pointed out that the ordinance would make it almost impossible to keep sexual predators and voyeurs out of women's restrooms. In fact, many opponents of the ordinance began calling it the "Sexual Predator Protection Act," and they petitioned to have the ordinance placed on the ballot for the citizens to decide. The city denied the petition—and city attorneys, at the direction of Houston's openly lesbian mayor—subpoenaed transcripts of sermons from pastors of Houston churches. It was a blatant violation of the First Amendment and a raw attempt to intimidate Houston pastors.

The subpoenas of the pastors' sermons quickly became a national news story, and the mayor reluctantly (but unrepentantly) withdrew the subpoenas. The measure was placed before the voters, who soundly defeated it. This incident shows that those who oppose biblical morality are ready to use unconstitutional intimidation tactics to place the church in a straitjacket and to muzzle the Christian conscience.

I can't peer into the motives of this lesbian mayor or the members of the Houston City Council. But I'm convinced that in many cases where government officials try to silence Christians, these actions spring from the willful, rebellious spirit of the City of Man. Oftentimes, I'm sure, the consciences of these officials must burn within them. They may believe their only motivation is to keep certain minorities from being discriminated against—but I believe some of them, deep down, are like Cain, filled with guilt, anxiety, and restlessness. That is why they build cities and cultures that defy God.

The City of Man is filled with momentary pleasures and noisy entertainment to distract the city dwellers from the pain of a burning conscience. The City of Man has bright lights and loud music so that those who dwell there don't have to face the emptiness of their lives. The City of Man offers thousands of ways to kill time so that people don't notice that time is killing them. The City of Man serves alcohol and mind-altering drugs so that people can numb the pain and shame of their guilt.

So if you come to the City of Man and stir up the conscience of those who live there, if you remind them of the meaninglessness of their lives, if you provoke their sense of shame and guilt, if you speak to them of their need for God—then be prepared for their rage. Don't take their hostility personally; they are taking out on you what they want to say to God.

Keep speaking the truth in love. Stand firm and don't budge from the truth—but always be gracious and kind. God says your reward in heaven will be great (Matthew 5:12; Luke 6:23).

PLEDGE ALLEGIANCE TO THE CITY OF GOD

Genesis 4:16 tells us that Cain went out from the Lord's presence and lived in the land of Nod. In the Hebrew language, *Nod* literally means "the land of wandering."[2] Those who try to make a virtue of their sin, thinking they can escape from the presence of God, will end up wandering without any place to call home.

When Israel wandered away from God and refused to repent, ignoring the warnings of one prophet after another, God finally said, "I'm going to take my hands off of Israel—and I will allow the Babylonians to come into the nation and do what they will." And you know the rest of the story.

God wanted to embrace Israel, bless Israel, and reason with Israel. But God's people refused to reason with Him. They fled from Him and figuratively wandered in the land of Nod. They refused to turn back to God.

Many in the church today refuse to turn back to God and reason with Him. They are practically daring God to invoke a new Babylonian Exile. When God removes His hand and the next global disaster strikes, there will be a calamity such as nothing the world has ever seen before. The economic devastation will make the Great Depression seem like a minor fiscal blip. The social upheaval, race wars, crime, and terrorism that result may be far beyond the control of even martial law.

When Rome fell, the Western world was plunged into a thousand years of darkness. It is impossible to predict what would happen if our own Western civilization fell. But we may live to find out.

That is why I appeal to you, as a sojourner in the City of Man, that you make sure that your allegiance to the City of God is undivided and uncompromised. Make sure that as you live in the City of Man, you maintain your wholehearted fidelity to the City of God. In these days, when many who profess to be Christians are selling out to and compromising with the culture, we must stand with Joshua, who said, "As for me and my household, we will serve the LORD" (Joshua 24:15).

God has strategically placed you in your neighborhood, your workplace, your campus, or your military base so that you can be an ambassador for the City of God, even though you now live in the City of Man. God does not call us to run from the City of Man or to hide in a bunker to wait out the Apocalypse. God has called us to stand in the thick of the fray, to plant our feet at the bloody crossroads of history, and to proclaim the good news to a dying world.

God calls us to invite others—before it's too late!—to come to the City of God. We cannot invite others to follow Jesus if we are living as they do. If our lives reflect anxiety and fear instead of confidence and faith, then what "good news" do we offer the world?

You represent the City of God while here in the City of Man. If you sense Him calling you, if you need to confess your sins, if you need to repent, if you need to turn to Him for forgiveness, you can do so today, right now.

Don't spend another moment lost in the City of Man. Spend eternity in the presence of the Lord Jesus, in the City of God.

7

CONFUSION
AND COLLAPSE

THE BATACLAN THEATRE in central Paris opened in February 1865. Designed in an imitation of Chinese architecture, the Bataclan is painted in bright, happy patterns of red, yellow, and white. Over the decades, a vast array of performers has appeared there, from Buffalo Bill Cody and his Wild West show to the rock bands Metallica and Guns N' Roses. But on November 13, 2015, the Bataclan theatre became a death chamber.

That night, as part of a series of terrorist attacks across Paris, three French gunmen of Algerian descent entered the Bataclan during a packed rock show. Heavily armed and wearing suicide belts, they went to the mezzanine, overlooking the concert crowd. Then, with shouts of "Allahu Akbar!"

("Allah is great!"), they opened fire on the people below. They reloaded several times, threw hand grenades, and took hostages.

Soon, French tactical units arrived and determined that the terrorists were killing hostages. So they launched an assault, shooting one of the terrorists. The other two died by triggering their suicide vests. In all, the attack left eighty-nine people dead and more than two hundred wounded.

For eight months, the French government suppressed the truth about what happened inside the Bataclan that night. Many victims were so badly mutilated that the government wouldn't release the bodies to the families. Initially, the government claimed the mutilating wounds were caused by shrapnel.

Then, in July 2016, the government revealed that, in addition to using bullets and bombs, the terrorists also gouged eyes, castrated men and shoved their testicles in their mouths, stabbed women in the genitals, and beheaded several victims. The terrorists recorded video of these horrors, planning to send the video to ISIS for recruitment and propaganda use. One police investigator who saw the bodies rushed out weeping and vomiting. For months, the French government had denied "rumors" of torture in the Bataclan attack. But the rumors were true.[1]

Terror struck the country again on Bastille Day, July 14, 2016, in Nice, in the south of France. After the fireworks show, an Islamist terrorist aimed a heavy truck-trailer rig at a crowd of some thirty thousand people on the Promenade des Anglais. For more than a mile, he mowed down everyone in his path, killing more than eighty people and injuring more than two hundred. Afterward, French prime minister Manuel Valls angered French citizens by declaring a state of helplessness, saying, "France is going to have to live with terrorism."[2]

Less than two weeks later, on July 26, 2016, two teenage jihadists pledged allegiance to ISIS and then entered a Normandy church where a Catholic priest, eighty-five-year-old Father Jacques Hamel, was celebrating Mass, along with two nuns and two parishioners. The two young men seized the priest and slashed his throat. As the elderly priest lay dying in his own blood, the teenagers turned to the nuns and did something totally unexpected: they *smiled*. They seemed happy and calm after killing the priest—and they were in no hurry to leave.

For the next few minutes, the two young barbarians engaged the nuns, Sister Huguette Peron and Sister Helene Decaux, in a discussion of comparative religions. They talked about the Quran. One of the nuns said that she had read the Quran and especially liked the suras (chapters) that spoke of peace.

"Peace," one of the murderers said. "That's what we want. As long as there are bombs [being dropped] on Syria, we will continue our attacks. And they will happen every day. When you stop, we will stop."

The conversation turned to the fear of death. One of the nuns said she didn't fear death, because she had faith in God and knew she would be happy in heaven with Jesus. One of the killers countered with a core doctrine of Islam— a doctrine that attacks the essence of the Christian gospel. "Jesus cannot be God and a man," he said. "It is you who are wrong."[3]

Minutes later, as the two young jihadists were preparing to escape by using the nuns and parishioners as human shields, the police burst in through a side door. Police officers opened fire, and the two teenage barbarians died.

THE COLLAPSE OF CHRISTIANITY

Father Mark A. Pilon, an American priest writing at a Catholic blog site, has observed that the collapse of Christianity all across Europe has left the people and governments of that continent unable to understand the growing threat of political Islam. He wrote:

> The dramatic loss of Christian faith in Europe is historically unprecedented. While some countries are slightly better off than others, the continent as a whole can no longer be described as a Christian civilization. . . .

Even the latest horror of the beheading of an 85-year-old priest in Normandy and the revelations of the brutal tortures of victims in the Bataclan Theater in Paris in November (finally leaked to the press), don't seem to have much raised understanding of the nature of the threat. . . .

Europe is now almost godless, an almost totally secularized continent with little or no spiritual dimension in the various nations that constitute the European Union.[4]

Lacking an understanding of the historic conflict between the Christian West and the Islamic East, Pilon explained, the leaders of Europe today are in the same state of cultural and spiritual blindness that Jesus described in Matthew 13:13—"though seeing, they do not see; though hearing, they do not hear or understand." Western leaders don't realize they face an existential threat from an ancient enemy: "the revival of a militant and determined form of extreme Islam bent upon, at long last, the domination of this formerly Christian continent."[5]

A Christian army stopped the conquering armies of Islam at the gates of Vienna in 1683. That victory quelled the Islamic threat to Christianity and Western civilization for about three centuries. But in recent years, the barbaric Islamists have returned to the battlefield. They have declared the entire Western world as their battleground—and their objective.

The Islamist threat to the West is as real today as it was centuries ago, yet our political and social leaders don't seem to know it. With every terror attack, our leaders look but do not see and hear but do not listen. They are culturally and spiritually blind. The apostle Paul aptly described the spiritual blindness of today's leaders: "The god of this age has blinded the minds of unbelievers, so that they cannot see the light of the gospel that displays the glory of Christ, who is the image of God" (2 Corinthians 4:4).

Being secularized and antireligious, Pilon says, Western leaders "simply cannot understand what they are seeing; that is, they cannot understand the kind of religious motivation that is behind the terror attacks, a deep religious conviction that believes in total war and the inevitability of a world domination."[6]

THE ULTIMATE THREAT TO WESTERN CIVILIZATION

The ultimate threat to Western civilization does not come from Islamist terrorism but from disturbing demographics: Europeans are having children at far below the replacement level and are losing population. The large-scale Muslim immigration into Europe, combined with the trend of large families among Muslim immigrants, guarantees that Western culture will retreat in the face of swelling numbers of Muslims in Europe. And Western civilization may well be defeated at the ballot box. If current trends continue, it's just a matter of time before Islam becomes the dominant culture, religion, and political system throughout Europe.

The farther our Western civilization drifts from our biblical roots, the deeper we plunge into confusion, fear, and blindness. The danger is upon us. The barbarians are already here—yet as a society, we still don't realize the very real threat that confronts us. The Islamists are not only bent on conquering our land. They also seek to conquer our minds and our souls. They want to eradicate the Christian gospel.

So they commit the most horrifying atrocities imaginable against so-called infidels, performing acts of torture that you and I could never imagine doing to another human being. Our minds recoil as we picture the scenes of horror inside the Bataclan theatre, on the streets of Nice, or in the church at Normandy. We don't want to even believe such barbaric acts are possible—yet they are happening with increasing frequency.

It's easy to fall into the trap of simply complaining about the gathering darkness of this dying world. I know. I have made the same complaints myself.

But we who know and love the Lord Jesus Christ are citizens of the City of God. We should never allow terrorism and other events to break our spirits or weaken our commitment to spreading the good news of Jesus Christ. As the darkness of barbarian terrorism grows, we should seize this opportunity to shine the light of God's love even more brightly than ever before.

FROM CAIN TO LAMECH

So far in this book we have been tracing the biblical account of the two contrasting humanities that formed two cities— the City of God and the City of Man. In chapter 6 we saw how Cain tried to make his own religion, offering a sacrifice to God according to his own will instead of the will of God. After God rejected Cain's offering and accepted the offering of his brother Abel, Cain murdered Abel—then he fled from the presence of God to build his own city, the first City of Man.

Continuing that narrative, we find that rebellious Cain was the father of a line of descendants. In the sixth generation from Cain, we meet Cain's descendant Lamech. In just a few sentences, the Word of God defines Lamech as a violent, rebellious, and self-centered man. Genesis 4:19 tells us that he married two women and became the first known polygamist in history. In verses 23–24, Scripture records Lamech's "Song of the Sword":

> Lamech said to his wives,
>> "Adah and Zillah, listen to me;
>>> wives of Lamech, hear my words.

I have killed a man for wounding me,
   a young man for injuring me.
If Cain is avenged seven times,
   then Lamech seventy-seven times."

In other words, Lamech was boasting to his wives of his violent and vengeful temper. In the original language, it is clear that Lamech was saying that a man struck him with his fist, and Lamech responded by running him through with the sword. He boasted that if anyone injured him in any way, he would repay that injury seventy-seven times over.

That is the bitter, vengeful, and violent mind-set of the City of Man. That is the legacy of Lamech's murderous ancestor, Cain.

But there is another man descended from Adam who represents the City of God. His name is Enoch. After Cain killed Abel and ran away, Adam and Eve had another son. His name was Seth, and Enoch was his descendant, born six generations from Seth. Enoch was as godly as Lamech was ungodly. Enoch illustrates the contrast between those who belong to the City of God and those who belong to the City of Man.

Enoch personifies the City of God. The book of Genesis tells us something truly amazing about Enoch: "Altogether, Enoch lived a total of 365 years. Enoch walked faithfully with God; then he was no more, because God took him away"

(Genesis 5:23–24). Does that really mean what it seems to mean? Did Enoch live such a godly life that he didn't have to pass through physical death but was instead translated straight into heaven? Yes.

Hebrews 11:5 tells us, "By faith Enoch was taken from this life, so that he did not experience death: 'He could not be found, because God had taken him away.' For before he was taken, he was commended as one who pleased God."

From Cain's rebellious offspring came Lamech—a violent, vengeful, self-willed man. From Seth's godly line came Enoch—a faithful believer who was spared the experience of death. Lamech was of the offspring of the serpent. Enoch was of the offspring of the woman—representing the godly line of descendants that would eventually lead to Jesus Christ. Enoch feared God and walked with God. And he belonged to the City of God.

FROM NOAH TO BABYLON

The demarcation between those who belong to the City of God and those who belong to the City of Man becomes even more obvious following the flood of Noah's day. A godly man who was a descendant of faithful Enoch, Noah was a preacher of righteousness, living in a time of great wickedness. God warned Noah of the judgment that was coming upon the earth, and He gave Noah detailed instructions to build the ark. By obeying God and seeking refuge in the ark,

Noah and his family were saved. His three sons, Shem, Ham, and Japheth, were saved as well.

But in these three sons, we see once again the contrast between the City of God and the City of Man. Genesis 9:20–27 tells the story of how Noah's son Ham sinned against his father. As a result, Ham's son Canaan was cursed—a curse that would remain on Canaan's descendants.

This story is a stark reminder that if you are living in the home of your parents, under their authority, you should obey them and honor them. If you are older, and on your own, then you are no longer under your parents' authority, but I still urge you to honor and respect your parents.

Children who obey their parents—and young adults who honor their parents—receive a blessing that is passed down, generation by generation. The Bible says, "Children, obey your parents in the Lord, for this is right. 'Honor your father and mother'—which is the first commandment with a promise—'so that it may go well with you and that you may enjoy long life on the earth'" (Ephesians 6:1–3).

Noah's other two sons, Shem and Japheth, honored their father, and as a result, they received the blessing that their brother Ham forfeited for his descendants.

What was the result of the curse on Ham's son Canaan? He dwelled in the City of Man. Canaan's brother Cush was the father of Nimrod—a man who took rebellion and defiance against God to new depths. Nimrod was a hunter, a warrior, and a builder of cities, and every one of the cities Nimrod built became an enemy of God and His people. The cities of Nimrod were centers of idolatry and astrology and occultism.

By looking at the works of Nimrod, we can easily discover his mind-set. His attitude toward God was one we often hear in our Western society today: *Why should I obey God? Why should I care what God says? What are God's moral laws to me? I am the captain of my own soul. My will is sovereign, and I don't answer to the will of God.*

The book of Genesis tells us:

> Cush was the father of Nimrod, who became a mighty warrior on the earth. He was a mighty hunter before the LORD; that is why it is said, "Like Nimrod, a mighty hunter before the LORD." The first centers of his kingdom were Babylon, Uruk, Akkad and Kalneh, in Shinar. From that land he went to Assyria, where he built Nineveh, Rehoboth Ir, Calah and Resen, which is between Nineveh and Calah— which is the great city. (10:8–12)

You may recognize the names of a few of those cities. Over the centuries, Israel repeatedly had conflict with the armies of those cities—especially Babylon. Did you realize that the wicked city of Babylon was founded by the great-grandson of Noah? Nimrod, the son of Cush, the grandson of Ham, a great-grandson of Noah, built the city of Babylon as an act of defiance against God.

Do you see now the clear contrast that God draws in His Word between the City of God and the City of Man? In both the Old Testament and the New Testament, the city of Babylon serves as a symbol of the City of Man—and the city of Jerusalem symbolizes the City of God. The Lord sent an unmistakable message to the rebellious people of Israel when He used Nebuchadnezzar, the king of Babylon, as an instrument of destruction against the rebellious people of Jerusalem. Babylon is a symbol of all those, in every era of history, who oppose God. Jerusalem is a symbol of all those who fear God and serve Him.

In Revelation 21, John sees a vision of the new City of God—the New Jerusalem. It is not the old, earthly Jerusalem but a brilliant, shining, gemlike city that comes down from heaven:

> He carried me away in the Spirit to a mountain great and high, and showed me the Holy City, Jerusalem, coming down out of heaven from God. It shone with the glory of God, and its brilliance was like that of a very precious jewel, like a jasper, clear as crystal. . . .
>
> The city does not need the sun or the moon to shine on it, for the glory of God gives it light, and the

Lamb is its lamp. The nations will walk by its light, and the kings of the earth will bring their splendor into it. On no day will its gates ever be shut, for there will be no night there. The glory and honor of the nations will be brought into it. Nothing impure will ever enter it, nor will anyone who does what is shameful or deceitful, but only those whose names are written in the Lamb's book of life. (Revelation 21:10–11, 23–27).

The glorious New Jerusalem is the ultimate victory and reward for all who belong to the City of God.

8

THE PATTERN OF BABYLON

THE CITY OF MAN—represented in the Bible as Babylon—always degenerates. It proceeds along a downward path of corruption and destruction. It takes a posture of opposition to God—then hardens that opposition into a stance of absolute hostility and rage. Often someone who begins as an agnostic eventually hardens into an atheist, then intensifies into an implacable foe of God and His people. Evil does not stand still—it always progresses toward greater and greater evil.

God has repeatedly and mercifully rescued Western civilization from its enemies. He gave the Christian army of King John III Sobieski of Poland the victory over the armies of Islam in 1683. He gave George Washington and the other Founding Fathers the victory over British tyranny and oppression in 1776. God gave Abraham Lincoln and the Union forces the victory over the slaveholding South in 1865. He gave the Allied forces, the defenders of Western civilization, the victory over Nazism and Fascism in 1945. And He gave Dr. Martin Luther King Jr. the victory over the forces of Jim Crow and segregation in America.

Again and again, God has defended Western civilization from attack by barbarians, slave merchants, totalitarians, genocidal racists, and segregationists. But instead of thanking God for His mercy and protection, we have taken all the credit for those victories. Instead of giving glory to God, we give the credit to . . .

secularism

materialism

multiculturalism

pluralism

political correctness

feminism

the welfare state

moral relativism

progressivism

environmentalism

atheism

humanism

Western civilization used to acknowledge and honor God. All the great institutions of the West were constructed on a foundation of faith in God. All the great universities in the West were founded by the church. Most of the great Western scientists and artists and statesmen—from Isaac Newton to Leonardo da Vinci to William Wilberforce—were devout believers. America, the centerpiece of Western civilization, was founded on a godly principle: "We hold these truths to be self-evident, that all men are created equal, that they are endowed by their Creator with certain unalienable Rights . . ."

Today, our universities have become strongholds of atheism and secularism. Our science, our art, and our laws are being used to marginalize and discredit the Christian faith. And America, founded on belief in an omniscient, omnipotent Creator, has banished God from every aspect of public life. Western civilization is being undermined from within, like a once-great edifice now being slowly but steadily consumed by termites.

I can already hear some people reading this book, wanting to slam it shut and say, "Michael, just leave me alone to enjoy my life! I don't want to know what's going on in the world. I can't handle the truth in these pages. I just want to keep my head in the sand and pretend that everything is going to turn out all right."

If that's how you feel, I understand. I wish I didn't have

to write about the horrible atrocities committed by the barbarians in our midst. I, too, often wish I could live inside a comfortable cocoon where nothing bad ever happens.

But I believe it's better to be prepared for the coming challenges than to be blindsided by them. I believe it's better to recognize our enemy—Satan—than to be ambushed by him. It's better to be vigilant citizens of the City of God than to be victims of the City of Man.

THE MYSTERY OF BABYLON

Nimrod built the city of Babylon as a fortress of opposition and defiance against the God who had saved his grandfather and great-grandfather from the Flood. In that city, the people planned an immense construction project—a tower that would be connected to heaven, the Tower of Babel.

Like so many people today, the ancient Babylonians didn't want to reach heaven *God's way*. They wanted to reach heaven *their way*. Genesis 11:4 describes the Tower of Babel—but most English translations mistake the meaning of that verse:

> Then they said, "Come, let us build ourselves a city, with a tower that reaches to the heavens, so that we may make a name for ourselves; otherwise we will be scattered over the face of the whole earth."

Many people today read that verse and think, *Oh, those ignorant, primitive Babylonians! They actually thought they could build a tower thousands or millions of miles high to reach the heavens!* But that's not what Genesis tells us.

The Babylonians were building a civilization, and their plan was to make God—the God of their ancestors, the God of Adam and Noah—obsolete. They were building a civilization that would oppose and reject God. They were building a civilization that would have no need for God. They intended the Tower of Babel to be a monument to their own genius. They began the Babel project as a way of making a name for themselves and establishing their fame worldwide.

They replaced the worship of God with the worship of the self. As a result, Babylon came to occupy a significant place in the Bible. The importance of Babylon in the outline of biblical history cannot be exaggerated. Throughout the entire Bible, Babylon is a symbol of living for oneself— and living at enmity with God.

That's why, when God's judgment fell on Israel because of the spiritual defection of the people, God chose the Babylonians as the instrument of His judgment. What was the religion of Nebuchadnezzar, the king of Babylon? He deified himself. He was a narcissist. He demanded that everyone in the kingdom bow to and worship an image of himself.

Now, what is the most prominent characteristic of the

coming Antichrist, as he is portrayed in the prophetic passages of the Bible? He is a narcissist. He has an image of himself set up in the temple in Jerusalem—what the prophet Daniel called an "abomination that causes desolation" (Daniel 9:27). The Antichrist then demands that everyone throughout the world bow to that image and worship the Antichrist (Revelation 13:14–15).

So the narcissism of Nebuchadnezzar, the king of Babylon, is a foreshadowing of the even greater narcissism of the coming Antichrist. No wonder Babylon came to represent, throughout the Bible, human self-worship and enmity with the one true God.

Do you see where we are now as a society? We are repeating the pattern of Babylon—the worship of the self and enmity with God. Western civilization is becoming Babylon, the City of Man—a city that rejects the one true God, a city that has stolen God's glory, a city dedicated to the deification and worship of man.

In Europe, in America, and throughout Western civilization, society is rejecting God, erasing Him from the public square, and replacing His gospel with secularism, pluralism, and all the other isms that are tearing at the fabric of our society. As our civilization declines, extreme political Islam has risen up to challenge our dying culture. And terrorism is now our lot.

Our civilization is aligning itself with the sin and idolatry of Babylon, just as Israel once aligned itself with the sin and idolatry of the surrounding culture. Whenever a civilization exchanges the worship of God for the idolatry of the self, fear and terror ensue. As we align ourselves with Babylon, we invite God to judge us exactly as He judged ancient Israel—

Exile.

The exile of rampant terrorism.

BABYLON IN THE LAST DAYS

The apostle John, in the book of Revelation, described the emergence of a symbolic Babylon in the Last Days:

> The woman was dressed in purple and scarlet, and was glittering with gold, precious stones and pearls. She held a golden cup in her hand, filled with abominable things and the filth of her adulteries. The name written on her forehead was a mystery:
>
> BABYLON THE GREAT
>
> THE MOTHER OF PROSTITUTES
>
> AND OF THE ABOMINATIONS OF THE EARTH.
>
> I saw that the woman was drunk with the blood of God's holy people, the blood of those who bore testimony to Jesus.

When I saw her, I was greatly astonished. (Revelation 17:4–6)

What is the mystery of Babylon that John was speaking of? Why did he call Babylon "the mother of prostitutes" and indeed, the mother of all the "abominations of the earth"? The mystery of Babylon refers to any household, any community, any church, any denomination, any city, any nation, any civilization that rejects God's moral absolutes and lives by an invented morality, a contrived spirituality, a man-made religion. In other words, the mystery of Babylon refers to the rejection and replacement of God and His Word.

What message did God give His people Israel when He sent the Babylonians to conquer them and take them captive? He was telling them, "You should have known better than to follow false gods. The pagans hate Me and reject Me, yet you want to be like them. Very well, I am removing My hand of protection from you. The Babylonians—the very people who hate Me and defy Me—will now come against you and take you into exile."

What do you think God is saying to us today through the rise of the barbarians? Is He once again saying, "You have rejected Me"? Will He remove His hand of protection from us? Will He send those who hate Him and reject Him against us? Will we one day look in the face of a young jihadist as he says to us, "Jesus cannot be God and a man. It is you who are wrong"? Is this how God must get our attention, so that we will repent?

Perhaps, as we have seen, the Muslim youth wearing a suicide vest provides us with the answer to these questions. The rise of barbaric, Islamist terrorism is God's judgment on Western civilization—and our own form of Babylonian Exile.

THE FALSE RELIGION OF ASTROLOGY

All the false gods of Egypt, Greece, Rome, and India originated in Babylon. The Babylonians invented those gods as alternatives to the one true God, the God they had rejected. The Tower of Babel was a ziggurat—a huge terraced pyramid that served as a temple complex for the worship of the false Babylonian gods. It is obvious that the Babylonians never intended the Tower of Babel to *literally* reach heaven. If they had wanted to do so, they would have built the tower on a mountain, not in the Mesopotamian valley.

The Tower of Babel was an aid to the Babylonians' study of astrology, their study of the supposed meaning of the signs in the stars. They believed that the stars could give them insight for their daily lives. Astrology—the practice of divining information about earthly events from the motions of the stars—originated in Babylon.

From Babylon, the occult religion of astrology was exported to Egypt. There it was combined with animism and other false religious practices, and it influenced the building of the pyramids and of the Sphinx. The pyramids of Egypt were constructed mathematically according to certain geometric relationships to the stars. Even the Sphinx has astrological significance. It depicts the head of a woman, symbolizing Virgo, the first sign of the zodiac. It has the body of a lion, symbolizing Leo, the last sign of the zodiac.

This ancient false religion has been revived in Western culture. Today, millions of Westerners plan their lives by the signs of the zodiac. One of the most famous people in recent memory to rely on astrology was Nancy Reagan, the late First Lady. After President Ronald Reagan was shot and nearly killed by an assassin's bullet in March 1981, Mrs. Reagan became obsessed with protecting her husband from harm.

In her memoir *My Turn*, Mrs. Reagan said that she called an astrologer, Joan Quigley, and told her, "I'm scared every time he leaves the house." Many people, unfortunately, are prone to magical thinking—believing they can affect events by consulting with the stars. Because Nancy Reagan was President Reagan's closest adviser, she had a great deal of control over his appointments and his schedule. So she would consult Joan Quigley for advice on everything from when Mr. Reagan should conduct arms-control talks with Mikhail Gorbachev to the removal of cancerous growths from Mr. Reagan's nose.[1]

Now, I believe Ronald Reagan was a devout Christian,

and I know that some people reading this book would rather not read that his wife was caught up with this ancient false religion of astrology. But the facts are what they are, and I need to state clearly that Christians should never consult horoscopes or involve themselves in any other occult practices. Why? Because astrology is the work of Satan.

Whether people know it or not, when they consult a horoscope or seek advice from an astrologer, they are dabbling with satanic forces. The Babylonians were inspired by Satan when they stole God's glory and gave it to themselves. In fact, by deifying themselves, they were truly giving glory to Satan.

SATAN'S PLAN B

When Satan failed to persuade Adam and Eve to worship him, he came up with Plan B—the Babylonians. The Babylonians created a religious system in which a man, King Nebuchadnezzar, was glorified above God. They built the city with a tower—a temple for the worship of the stars. Why? "So that we may make a name for ourselves" (Genesis 11:4).

You might say, "Michael, I see how sinful it was for Nebuchadnezzar to set up an image of himself and demand to be worshipped. But what does that have to do with me? I don't worship myself—and I don't demand that other people worship me."

Well, let me ask you this: How much of God's gift of time do you give back to Him? How much of God's gift of money do you give back to Him? How much of God's gifts of your talent, your intellect, your thoughts, and your devotion do you give back to Him?

Today in America, the god of Self reigns supreme. There is even a magazine called *Self*, printed so that twelve times a year, you can read about all the many ways you can pamper yourself, celebrate yourself, and worship yourself. The god of Self is alive and well and reigning over our society. And because so many people worship at the altar of the Self, we are under God's judgment, and that judgment has taken the form of Islamic terrorism.

The god of Self has even invaded the church. Have you listened to preachers who treat the ministry of the gospel as a form of entertainment? There is very little in their preaching that you could call solid biblical wisdom—but there is a lot of entertainment. And much of the music in churches today seems to be focused on entertaining the crowd, not feeding the soul.

Be on your guard against the god of Self. The idolatry of the Self is subtle. The idolatry of the Self is easily rationalized. The idolatry of the Self can make us feel warm and tingly inside. But the idolatry of the Self is the religion of Babylon. It is a satanic religion.

THE ULTIMATE VICTORY

Our God is a jealous God—not jealous in the sense of a sinful envy, but rather in the sense of a protective love (Exodus 34:14). He does not want to share us with idols and false religions. He loves us so much that He wants us all to Himself. He will not simply shrug and let us go our own way when we are unfaithful to Him. God will not tolerate rivals when it comes to His bride.

When the Babylonians made plans to build their own doorway to heaven at the Tower of Babel, God—the Holy Trinity—took counsel and said, "Come, let us go down and confuse their language so they will not understand each other" (Genesis 11:7). And confusion was the fate of the Babylonians.

God is very patient with us, but a day eventually comes when He says, "Enough is enough." Make no mistake about it; God always prevails. He always has the last word. God always achieves His purpose. So we need to make sure that our lives are aligned with His purpose.

We have never lived in more confused and bewildering times. One example of that confusion was the election in May 2016 of an Islamist, Sadiq Khan, as the mayor of London. Why did Londoners elect a man with close ties to Islamic supremacists and anti-Semites? There are 1.3 million Muslims in London, a city of 8.5 million people[2]—

but though Muslims are a sizable minority, and though voter fraud was reported in Muslim precincts, Muslim support alone could not have elected Mr. Khan.

Khan's election can be explained by the attitude of the large number of non-Muslim voters in London. The city of London is overwhelmingly populated by liberals and progressives who like to show how "enlightened" they are by electing candidates at the extreme end of the spectrum—and that includes Muslims. By electing a Muslim, liberal-progressive voters are saying, "See how wonderfully enlightened we are? We're not prejudiced against Muslims. We just elected one as our mayor!"

After the election of Mr. Khan, London buses carried large advertising placards proclaiming, "Subḥān Allāh! Glory be to Allah!"[3] It was a celebration of yet another victory in the gradual Islamization of Great Britain.

That is confusion. That is twisted, mixed-up thinking. We in Western civilization are actually voting for and celebrating the demise of our own culture. We are making deals with the Islamists to give away our civilization. This is cultural suicide.

The demented people who are so desperate to be thought of as "enlightened" may one day wake up and realize that by tossing away their history and tradition and culture, they have surrendered something incredibly valuable—something they can never regain. Once Sharia law is voted in by an

Islamist majority, all of the so-called enlightened people will have to submit to Islamic rule.

But let me give a word to the faithful—to those who are citizens of the City of God, living in the City of Man: No matter how dark and frightening the world becomes, our God is a God of power and might. He will win the ultimate victory, and those of us who belong to God will share in it. No matter how the world may hate us and hurt us and persecute us, we will be victorious in Jesus's name.

9

THE CLASH OF CULTURES

AMERICANS HAVE A HARD TIME understanding why Islamic extremists hate us so much. After all, America has often reached out to Muslim people in a spirit of friendship and has defended Muslims from attacks and oppression. America helped arm the mujahideen ("army of jihadists") against the Soviet occupation of Afghanistan. America defended Bosnian Muslims against genocidal attacks by Serbs in the former Yugoslavia, and we defended ethnic Albanians against Serbian genocide in Kosovo. We liberated Kuwait and Iraq from the tyrannical regime of Saddam Hussein. America and its NATO allies helped liberate Libya from Muammar Gaddafi.

In spite of all the blood and treasure America has sacrificed to defend Muslims, the Islamists still want to do us harm. They don't just hate our government. They hate *us*—and for a variety of reasons. They remember how Western nations colonized and exploited the Arab world. They believe America's economic success is the result of greed and political oppression. They hate America's support for Israel. They hate the immorality in our entertainment media.

Osama bin Laden once described the conflict between Islam and the West as a war of true faith versus unbelief:

Our call is the call of Islam that was revealed to Muhammad. It is a call to all mankind. We have been entrusted with good cause to follow in the footsteps of the Messenger [Muhammad] and to communicate his message to all nations. It is an invitation that we extend to all the nations to embrace Islam, the religion that calls for justice, mercy and fraternity among all nations. . . . We are entrusted to spread this message and to extend that call to all the people. We, nonetheless, fight against their governments and all those who approve of the injustice they practice against us. We fight the governments that are bent on attacking our religion and on stealing our wealth and on hurting our feelings.[1]

Islam currently boasts about 1.6 billion adherents and is spreading faster than at any other time in history. It is the dominant religion in forty-nine nations.[2] Its spread has encouraged the rise of militant, political Islam—the original Islam of the seventh century.

Militant Islamists hate everything Christians stand for. They hate our freedom. They hate the gospel, which is blasphemy to them. The notion of a tolerant society that guarantees religious liberty is alien to their way of thinking, because they seek to bring the world into submission to Sharia law.

Militant Islamists view Christianity as the foremost foe of Islam for four basic reasons:

1. Islamists see Christianity as the primary expression of infidel wickedness. They mistakenly assume that Christian values pervade Western civilization the way Islamic ideology pervades the Muslim world. They don't understand the secularization and pluralism of Western society. So when Muslims see the immorality of Hollywood films, they blame Christianity.

2. Because of the history of the Crusades, Islamic extremists see Christianity as the most potent ideological threat they face. If Islam can conquer

Christianity, they reason, then all of Islam's other foes can be readily defeated.

3. Though Muslims regard Christianity as a potent enemy, they view individual Christians as soft, passive targets. They interpret our tolerance as a weakness that they can exploit to subjugate us. Westerners reinforce this impression by refusing to defend our culture.

4. Islamists blame the Christian West for many of the social ills of the Middle East, including poverty, ignorance, unrest, and oppression. They blame the West for corrupting Muslim culture with immoral movies and attire. And they blame the West for supporting Israel.

Violence-inclined Muslims find support in the Quran, which teaches, "Fight those who believe not in Allah nor the Last Day" (Quran 9:29), kill unbelievers who do not offer you peace—"slay them wherever ye catch them" (Quran 2:191; 4:91), and "take not the Jews and the Christians for your friends" (Quran 5:51). The Quran also says that Jews and Christians believe in idols and false worship (Quran 4:51), that Allah will not forgive those who believe in the Trinity (Quran 4:48; 28:62–64), and that Christians—those who believe that Jesus is God—will burn in hell (Quran 5:72). The Quran says that Christians are doomed to destruction for believing that Jesus is the Son of God (Quran 9:30; 19:35–37).

Western civilization was founded on Judeo-Christian beliefs. There is an unbridgeable gulf between those who embrace the faith of the Old and New Testaments and those who embrace, literally and fanatically, the most violent passages of the Quran. Political Islam and Sharia law do not permit coexistence with any other belief system, and especially not Judaism or Christianity.

Today, there is a clash between the cultures of the Christian West and the Islamic East that can be traced all the way back to the era of Islam's founder, Muhammad. Islamists have revived all the old hostilities, and they are at war against "Crusaders" and "infidels."

In a real sense, this culture clash can be traced long before the birth of Christ—to the time of the first patriarch, Abraham.

WAITING FOR THE NEW JERUSALEM

The story of Abraham begins in Genesis 11. He was born the son of a Chaldean man named Terah, who named him Abram. Joshua 24:2 tells us, "Terah the father of Abraham and Nahor, lived beyond the Euphrates River and worshiped other gods."

Some Bible scholars believe that, in his early life, Abram was an idolater like his father and that he converted to faith in the one true God when the Lord called him in Genesis 12. Other Bible scholars believe that Abram may have rejected his father's idolatrous beliefs and followed God from an early age—and God honored his faith by calling him into a new land. The Bible is silent on whether or not Abram (later renamed Abraham) followed God from an early age or was converted when God called him.

Abraham's home city, Ur, was located in the region we now know as southern Iraq, on the Euphrates River, about ten miles from the modern city of Nasiriyah. Ur was the center of worship of the Assyrian-Babylonian moon god known as Nanna. You can still visit the ruins of Ur today, including the partially restored ruins of the great Ziggurat of Ur, the shrine to the god Nanna. When Abraham departed from Ur, he left the center of pagan moon god worship to follow the one true God.

Ur was also the cultural and commercial center of the Mesopotamian world in Abraham's time. It was a highly advanced city with schools, libraries, and marketplaces. It was much like the culturally advanced Western world we live in today. It was the epitome of the City of Man in that era.

But Abraham did not want to be a part of the City of Man, no matter how much wealth, entertainment, and worldly enlightenment Ur had to offer. Abram married Sarai, and along with Abram's father, Terah, and nephew Lot, he left the city of Ur in the land of the Chaldeans and set off for Canaan. They stopped at a place called Harran and stayed for a while. After Abram's father died, God told Abram:

"Go from your country, your people and your father's household to the land I will show you.

"I will make you into a great nation,
   and I will bless you;
I will make your name great,
   and you will be a blessing.
I will bless those who bless you,
   and whoever curses you I will curse;
and all peoples on earth
   will be blessed through you." (Genesis 12:1–3)

So Abram set off for the promised land. He was seventy-five years old when he left Harran. When Abram reached the great tree of Moreh at Shechem, God appeared to Abram and said, "To your offspring I will give this land" (v. 7). So Abram built an altar to the Lord at that place. From there he went on to the hills east of Bethel, and he built an altar to God and called upon the name of the Lord.

The New Testament writer to the Hebrews offers an insight from the life of Abraham that applies to your life and mine:

By faith Abraham, when called to go to a place he would later receive as his inheritance, obeyed and went, even though he did not know where he was going. By faith he made his home in the promised land like a stranger in a foreign country; he lived in tents, as did Isaac and Jacob, who were heirs with him of the same promise. For he was looking forward to the city with foundations, whose architect and builder is God. (Hebrews 11:8–10)

Abraham knew what it was like to be caught in a clash of cultures. He was born into the idolatrous Chaldean culture, and his own father was an idol worshipper. Yet God reached into the life of this man Abraham, and he called Abraham out of that rebellious and ungodly culture with its false religious system. Though Abraham loved and respected his father, he would not go along with his father's idolatry. He remained until his father's death—and then he was free to go wherever God led him.

So Abraham made his way into the land of Canaan— and there, just as in Ur of the Chaldeans, Abraham encountered foreign cultures that practiced false religions. By faith, Abraham made his home in the promised land—but he didn't pour a concrete foundation and put up a permanent house. Instead, he sojourned in the promised land, like a stranger in a strange land. Abraham and his family lived in tents, and they were always ready to pack up and leave at a moment's notice. He knew that his descendants would be heirs of the promise God gave him, but Abraham himself would have to wait for a city with permanent foundations—a city "whose architect and builder is God" (Hebrews 11:10).

Abraham had to wait for the coming of the New Jerusalem. In fact, Abraham is *still* waiting for the New Jerusalem. God's Eternal City still lies in our future. Like Abraham, we await the arrival of the city whose architect and builder is God. And like Abraham, we live like strangers in a strange land. We know that this world is not our true home, so, for the time being, we are living as sojourners, in tents.

The hardest, most trying times of all are times of waiting. And this present time of waiting is made all the harder because we are engaged in a great struggle with the surrounding culture. We are caught, like Abraham, in a clash of cultures.

God had called Abraham, and he was looking forward to the City of God, a city with imperishable foundations, whose architect and builder is God Himself. Abraham was willing to spend the rest of his life as a stranger in a strange land, living in tents, waiting for the coming of the true City of God. And waiting. And waiting.

When we are forced to wait on God, year after year, we are tempted to doubt His promises. No one ever experienced a longer wait than Abraham. He was seventy-five years old when God promised he would have a son. He was one hundred when that son, Isaac, was born. So Abraham and his wife, Sarah, who were well into their golden years when the promise was given, waited twenty-five years before the promise of a son was fulfilled.

And Abraham waited *the rest of his life* for the promised land. He never received the fulfillment of that promise in his lifetime. Yet he never gave up waiting and believing.

There's an important lesson for you and me in the story of Abraham and his long wait for the fulfillment of God's promises. Ever since I committed my life to Christ, I have been waiting for the return of the Lord. I may not get to see the Lord's return with my physical eyes. I may pass through the portal of death before the Lord's return—but I will never stop waiting and expecting His return.

You may be waiting right now for the Lord to fulfill a promise He has made to you. You may have begun to doubt His promise. You may be ready to simply give up—but please don't. Keep trusting, expecting, and believing. God always keeps His promises.

GOD ALWAYS KEEPS HIS PROMISES

Adoniram Judson was a brilliant young man. Born in 1788, he entered the College of Rhode Island (now Brown University) at age sixteen and graduated as class valedictorian at nineteen. Raised in a Christian home, he abandoned the

Christian faith when an atheist classmate convinced him that God didn't exist.

A few years later, Judson was spending the night in a country inn—but the loud cries and moans of a sick man in the next room kept him awake through the night. The next morning, Judson went out to speak to the innkeeper and learned that the man in the next room had died. Judson was astonished to learn the identity of the dead man: it was the atheist classmate who had turned Judson away from his faith.

Adoniram Judson knew that it could not have been a random coincidence. God had deliberately placed him in the room next to the dying man—and Judson knew that God was trying to get his attention. So Judson dedicated himself to serving Christ for the rest of his life. He felt God calling him to be a missionary in Burma.

Judson and his wife arrived in Rangoon, Burma, in 1813. During his first seven years in that country, Judson made only one convert. After eleven years, he had made just eighteen converts—and during that eleventh year, war broke out between England and Burma. The Burmese government arrested Judson on suspicion of espionage. His captors marched him barefoot for miles and imprisoned him, starved him, and tortured him in one of the world's most notorious prisons. Finally, the Burmese government freed him—but only weeks after his release, his wife died.

Having lost his wife, and feeling he was a failure as a

missionary, Judson entered a year of suicidal depression. He was so despondent that he dug a grave next to his jungle hut and imagined himself lying down in the grave and never coming out. But after that terrible year of despondency, Judson began to feel the light of God's love filtering into his life once more, stirring his passion to share the gospel with the Burmese people.

In 1828, Adoniram Judson met a tribesman named Ko Tha Byu—a notorious murderer and robber. Judson led him to the Lord and baptized him—and Ko Tha Byu became a preacher and evangelist much like the apostle Paul. He took the gospel to his own people and began winning souls by the dozen.

It turned out that this Burmese tribe had a number of legends that were remarkably similar to the stories of the Old Testament. They believed in one eternal, omnipotent God, the Creator of the heavens and the earth. They had a legend that was remarkably similar to the story of Adam and Eve. They believed in a coming Messiah. They were well prepared to receive the gospel of Jesus Christ.

So this former murderer and robber—Adoniram Judson's only convert in that tribe—became a tireless evangelist and church planter. By the time Ko Tha Byu died in 1840, there were more than twelve hundred Christians in his tribe. The tribal church continued to grow long after his death.

Adoniram Judson came close to giving up on God's

promise—but he waited. It was after that terrible year of depression, when Judson was ready to step into a grave and never come out, that God threw open the doors to evangelizing the Burmese tribesmen. Adoniram Judson left an amazing legacy and a profound example for you and me. Whenever God calls you and gives you a promise, trust Him and wait on Him. The God of Abraham, the God of Adoniram Judson, always keeps His Word.

THE CITY NAMED "THE LORD IS THERE"

On a number of occasions, I have led people to Christ, and they have told me through tears, "My dear father, my dear mother, prayed for me and believed that I would one day come to Christ. I wish my parents were still here to see me make this decision. I'm sorry I waited until after they died— it would have given them so much joy to know I made this decision."

Don't quit praying for those loved ones who need to know the Lord Jesus. Keep praying, keep trusting God, keep believing—even if you never see your prayers answered in your lifetime. Genuine faith in the promise of God is deaf to doubt. Genuine faith in the promise of God is dumb to discouragement. Genuine faith in the promise of God is blind to impossibilities. Genuine faith refuses to give up or let go.

Abraham left the City of Man and looked forward to the City of God. No matter how many temptations he confronted, no matter how many years of discouragement he endured, he never took his eyes off God's promise of the City of God. Yes, he was a flawed human being. He sinned. He made mistakes. He tried to rush God's promise along. But in spite of his flaws, he kept his eyes on God's promise.

As the world grows darker, as the faith of those around us grows weaker, as our enemies grow stronger, we will be tempted to let go of our faith. We will be tempted to give in to discouragement and self-pity. That is why Paul implores us, "Set your minds on things above, not on earthly things" (Colossians 3:2).

Don't set your mind on the City of Man. Set your mind on the City of God. Look forward to that divine and eternal city—the same city Abraham waited for. This city is called by many names in the Bible, but I think the sweetest name of all is found in Ezekiel 48:35:

"And the name of the city from that time on will be: THE LORD IS THERE."

Of all the great and wonderful things we can know about this heavenly city, the greatest fact of all is that *the Lord is there*! So let us fix our eyes on this comforting promise, this amazing truth. Faith sees the invisible. Faith hears the inaudible. Faith touches the intangible. Faith accomplishes the impossible. And faith is not just wishful thinking—*faith is active.*

JERUSALEM—THE CITY OF PEACE

God in His grace has provided an earthly city that foreshadows the City of God. This earthly city is only a temporary provision where God's name is lifted up, where we sense the promise, yet unfulfilled, of God's peace here on earth. That is why this earthly city is called Jerusalem, the city of peace.

Though Jerusalem hardly seems like a city of peace today, it is the city where Melchizedek, the king of Salem and priest of El Elyon ("God Most High"), met Abraham with bread and wine and a blessing (Genesis 14:18–20).

That is why Abraham offered all that he had—including his only son of promise, Isaac—to God. According to 2 Chronicles 3:1–2, Mount Moriah, where Abraham was prepared to offer Isaac, is the Temple Mount, where Solomon built the temple of the Lord. And that is why Jesus was offered as a sacrifice in Jerusalem; with His death on the cross, He purchased our peace with God. When King David established Jerusalem as the center of worship for the nation of Israel, Jerusalem became a symbol, a foretaste, of the City of God.

Today, every faithful church, every faithful Sunday school, every faithful home Bible study, and every faithful Christian ministry is to be a place where God is uniquely present, where the Word of God is proclaimed, where the encouragement of God dwells, and where the peace of God reigns. The church on earth is to be a symbol, a foretaste, of the City of God. Like Jerusalem, the church is a temporary city, a foreshadow of the New Jerusalem that is to come.

FROM A CONDITIONAL PROMISE
TO UNCONDITIONAL BLESSING

King David was an imperfect king, to say the least. He committed adultery, then tried to cover up his sin with murder. He messed up—royally!

In spite of his sins and his crimes, King David had a deep desire to honor God, to worship God, and to live in the presence of God. Though he failed God, he repented and returned to serving God with all his might for the rest of his life. There's a lesson in the life of King David for you and me.

If you live in the City of Man, surrounded by its sin and darkness, yet you refuse to surrender to its allure . . .

If you choose to honor God in the face of all threats and hostility . . .

If you choose to exercise faith instead of giving in to fear . . .

If you choose to glorify God with your life, regardless of the cost or the consequences . . .

If you choose to bless the Lord in a world that curses His name . . .

. . . then, just as God overruled the sin of David, He will overrule your failures and sins. If you fail God but return to Him in genuine repentance and brokenness, then like David, you will be remembered as a man or woman after God's own heart.

The word *Zion* has often been used as a metaphor for the city of Jerusalem or the nation of Israel or even the believer's hope of heaven. But Mount Zion in the Old Testament is a specific place, a mountain ridge just south of the Temple Mount. It was the site of the Jebusite fortress that King David conquered and renamed the City of David (2 Samuel 5:6–10; 1 Chronicles 11:4–9). The book of Psalms contains a number of "psalms of Zion," which include such passages as:

> Great is the LORD, and most worthy of praise,
>> in the city of our God, his holy mountain.
>
> Beautiful in its loftiness,
>> the joy of the whole earth,
> like the heights of Zaphon is Mount Zion,
>> the city of the Great King.
> God is in her citadels;
>> he has shown himself to be her fortress. (Psalm 48:1–3)

God is renowned in Judah;
   in Israel his name is great.
His tent is in Salem,
   his dwelling place in Zion.
There he broke the flashing arrows,
   the shields and the swords, the weapons of war. (Psalm
   76:1–3)

He has founded his city on the holy mountain.
The LORD loves the gates of Zion
   more than all the other dwellings of Jacob.

Glorious things are said of you,
   city of God. (Psalm 87:1–3)

Again and again in the Psalms, Mount Zion is portrayed as the City of God, the city where God dwells. To be in Jerusalem, especially in the City of David, was to be in the City of God, in the presence of God. Yet the physical Mount Zion, the historic City of David, was only a foreshadowing of the true City of God, the New Jerusalem, where we will one day live forever, praising God.

Jerusalem was a temporary city, chosen by God's grace to symbolize and foreshadow the Eternal City of God. Jerusalem was a temporary city protected and sustained by conditional promises. God had promised to keep His hand of protection on that city as long as the people remained faithful to Him.

In Deuteronomy 28, God gave the people of Israel a promise—and a warning. He said:

> If you fully obey the LORD your God and carefully follow all his commands I give you today, the LORD your God will set you high above all the nations on earth. All these blessings will come on you and accompany you if you obey the LORD your God. . . .
>
> However, if you do not obey the LORD your God and do not carefully follow all his commands and decrees I am giving you today, all these curses will come on you and overtake you. . . . (Deuteronomy 28:1–2, 15)

God placed before Israel a conditional promise—a blessing and a curse. If the people followed the Lord's commands, then the nation would be blessed. If the people proved unfaithful and disobedient, then the curses would ensue. And as it turned out, the people wandered from God and brought down the curses upon themselves.

The people repeatedly brought these curses upon themselves during the time of the Judges. And they brought these curses upon themselves again in the Babylonian Exile. Finally, the people of Israel brought these curses upon themselves when they rejected and crucified the promised Messiah. At that moment, earthly Jerusalem ceased to be the city where God dwells. His conditional promise to Israel was, "If you reject Me, I will remove My presence from you."

That's why Jesus, shortly before His crucifixion, wept over Jerusalem, saying:

> If you, even you, had only known on this day what would bring you peace—but now it is hidden from your eyes. The days will come upon you when your enemies will build an embankment against you and encircle you and hem you in on every side. They will dash you to the ground, you and the children within your walls. They will not leave one stone on another, because you did not recognize the time of God's coming to you. (Luke 19:42–44)

Jesus wept over Jerusalem and prophesied its destruction. In AD 70, the Romans, led by General Titus, laid siege to the city, broke through the gates, slaughtered the people, razed the temple, and they did not leave one stone upon another. The tearstained prophecy of Jesus was fulfilled to the letter.

In the old Jerusalem, God's presence was limited and temporary. In the New Jerusalem, He will be eternally omnipresent. In the old Jerusalem, God's people were prone to wander. In the New Jerusalem, believers will worship Him in spirit and in truth. In the old Jerusalem, the people often turned to worldly pleasures. In the New Jerusalem, God's people will delight in Him. God's blessing on earthly Jerusalem was conditional. In the New Jerusalem, God's blessings will be unconditional, because no conditions will be needed. Thanks to the transforming grace of God, we will be like Jesus.

FOCUS ON THE HEAVENLY CITY

In these times, we live in the City of Man while awaiting the City of God. We are continually tempted to take our eyes off of the promised city that is to come. We are tempted by the lures and enticements of the City of Man. And all too many Christians in all too many churches have succumbed to those enticements, inviting God's judgment.

I believe that Jesus now weeps over many churches today, as He once wept over the city of Jerusalem. From pulpits where the good news of Jesus Christ was once proclaimed, unfaithful ministers now preach a scandalous tolerance for sin. God will not dwell among people who betray His message and reject His authority.

Great reformers and revivalists, such as John Knox and John and Charles Wesley, founded Christian denominations that once lifted up the name of Jesus above all else. Today those denominations seek friendship with the world. They preach a message designed to soothe the emotions and win popularity contests. They don't preach about the cross of Christ or the blood of Christ, because that would make people uncomfortable.

So the people who go to those churches no longer hear the gospel—they hear a message of feel-good platitudes designed only to keep the pews warm and the loose change jingling in the collection plates. Those churches are no longer part of the City of God. They have sold out to the City of Man.

Jesus reaffirmed the promise of the City of God when He told the Samaritan woman by Jacob's well:

A time is coming when you will worship the Father neither on this mountain nor in Jerusalem. You Samaritans worship what you do not know; we worship what we do know, for salvation is from the Jews. Yet a time is coming and has now come when the true worshipers will worship the Father in the Spirit and in truth, for they are the kind of worshipers the Father seeks. God is spirit, and his worshipers must worship in the Spirit and in truth. (John 4:21–24)

A day is coming when those who truly belong to the Lord will worship God not in an earthly city, which is a mere foreshadow, but in the New Jerusalem. That is why Abraham looked ahead to the city whose architect and builder is God. That is why nothing evil or sinful can dwell in it. When we finally dwell with God in that city, we will at last understand what it means for Jesus to be called Immanuel—"God with us" (Matthew 1:23).

Today, living in the City of Man, our vision is dim and our comprehension is clouded. Instead of clinging to God, we run from Him. Instead of remembering His blessings, we forget Him. Instead of listening for His voice, we stop up our ears.

We are continually distracted by the clash of cultures— the clash between the City of God and the City of Man. The City of Man shouts to us from our TVs, radios, computers, and smartphones, from our social media, our entertainment media, our news media, from our neighbors and coworkers, from our opinion leaders and our political leaders—and even, I have to say, from many of our church leaders. The babbling voices of the City of Man distract us from the still, small voice of the Spirit of God.

To hear God's voice, we may need to turn off our electronic devices and simply listen in prayer and meditation. We may need to withdraw from the clash of cultures so that we can experience the peace and serenity that comes from hearing the voice of God.

In the clash between the City of Man and the City of God, be sure you know which side you're on. Like Abraham, keep your eyes fixed on the heavenly city with everlasting foundations, whose architect and builder is God.

10

WARNING SIGNS OF IMPENDING JUDGMENT

JOHN KNOX WAS BORN in Scotland around 1513, and he began serving as a Catholic priest around 1540. After studying the claims of Martin Luther, John Calvin, and the other Reformers, he began to openly question dogmas of the Catholic Church such as the veneration of Mary, the mother of Jesus.

When a friend, Reformer George Wishart, was arrested by Catholic officials, Knox was ready to go to prison with him. Wishart persuaded him not to. "One is sufficient for a sacrifice," Wishart said. Wishart was later tried and burned at the stake by the Catholic Church. If not for Wishart's advice, Knox would have suffered the same fate.

John Knox became known as a great Reformation preacher who trusted God's Word as his sole authority. Salvation, he preached, was by grace through faith alone. He rejected all unbiblical beliefs and practices, including purgatory and prayers for the dead.

In 1547, a fleet of French galleys—sailing ships propelled by oarsmen—invaded Scotland and took a number of Protestants, including Knox, as prisoners. The Catholic French considered Protestants to be heretics, and heretics were, in their minds, fit only to be imprisoned or enslaved. So Knox and his fellow Protestants were chained to benches as galley slaves and forced to row the oars under the lash of a slave master.

After a year of imprisonment as a galley slave, Knox was ill nourished and often sick with fever. The French galleys returned to the Scottish coastline, scouting for ships to attack. Once, as the galley sailed past the village of St. Andrews, Knox saw the spires of the parish church where he had once preached. A fellow prisoner asked him if he recognized the place. Knox replied, "I know it well. That's the steeple of the kirk where I first preached. I'll not die until I have preached there again."

In 1549, after spending more than a year and a half as a galley slave, Knox was released. History does not record how he obtained his freedom, but we know he went to England, where the church under Archbishop of Canterbury Thomas

Cranmer was friendly toward Protestants. Knox preached in the reformed Church of England, and his simple gospel, rooted in Scripture alone, attracted many new people to his congregation. But when Mary Tudor was crowned queen and reestablished Roman Catholicism in England, Protestant preachers were endangered. Knox fled to Europe.

In 1559, Knox returned to Scotland, where he was declared an outlaw, subject to summary trial and execution. Undaunted, Knox returned to the church at St. Andrews and preached boldly, fulfilling the promise he had made as a galley slave.

The following year, the Scottish Parliament asked Knox and five other Reformed ministers to draw up a new confession of faith. The Scots Confession was critical not only of Catholicism but of the English Reformers who were content to have the queen of England as the head of the Lord's church.

In August 1561, eighteen-year-old Mary, Queen of Scots, arrived from France to take the throne of Scotland. The young queen had been in France since the age of five. A devout Catholic on the throne of Protestant Scotland, she knew almost nothing about the political and religious realities of the land she ruled.

When Knox preached a sermon critical of the Catholic Church and the Catholic monarch, Mary summoned Knox to the Palace of Holyroodhouse and accused him of inciting rebellion. The queen believed that a monarch had absolute authority over the conscience of the people. Knox insisted that monarchs are accountable to God and subject to the authority of Scripture.

So the preacher and the queen were on a collision course. Their conversation went much like this:

"Do you think," the queen asked, "that my authority as queen of Scotland is unjust?"

"I am content to live under Your Grace," Knox said, "as the apostle Paul was content to live under Nero. So long as you do not persecute Protestants, I will not oppose your authority. I am not opposed to you, but to that wicked Jezebel, the queen of England, being head of the Church of England."

"And yet," Mary said, "you have taught the people to receive another religion—Protestantism—which I cannot allow. How can that be a godly doctrine, since God commands subjects to obey their rulers?"

Mary was probably referring to Romans 13:1, where Paul wrote, "Let everyone be subject to the governing authorities, for there is no authority except that which God has established. The authorities that exist have been established by God." Or perhaps to 1 Peter 2:13–17, where Peter wrote, "Submit yourselves for the Lord's sake to every human authority. . . . Honor the emperor."

Knox replied, "Madam, rulers often ignore the Scriptures,

and there are numerous examples in the Old Testament to prove that subjects are not bound to obey an unjust and ungodly command by their rulers."

"You seem to be saying," Mary said, "that my subjects must obey you instead of me, and that I must do what my subjects command—and be subject to them and not they to me."

"God forbid," Knox replied, "that I would ever command anyone to obey me. I only want rulers and subjects to obey God. There is no humiliation for a monarch to submit to God's authority. By submitting to the will of God, rulers will gain everlasting blessing."

Mary said that the Roman Catholic Church was the true Church of God, to which John Knox replied that the Catholic Church, which he called "that Roman harlot," was corrupt. Their conversation went downhill from there.[1]

Sometime later, Mary, Queen of Scots, tried to have John Knox charged with treason, but Knox successfully defended himself before the Privy Council. Knox went on to serve as minister of the High Church of Edinburgh from 1560 until his death in 1572. Though Mary, Queen of Scots, wanted Knox beheaded, he died of natural causes—and it was Mary herself who was later beheaded (she was implicated in a plot against her cousin, Queen Elizabeth I).

At his funeral, John Knox was eulogized with these great words: "Here lies one who never feared any flesh."[2] A true citizen of the City of God, Knox lived and died standing for God's truth.

John Knox exemplifies a two-sided question that has raged from Old Testament times to this very day: What is the role of the government with regard to the church? And what is the role of believers in relationship to the government?

CORRUPTION IN THE GOVERNMENT— AND THE CHURCH

Whether you are a Republican, a Democrat, an Independent, or you align yourself with some third party, there is a good chance you may not like what I'm about to say. While it's never my intention to offend anyone, sometimes an offense cannot be helped. The truth itself often causes an offense.

In recent years, our American civilization has retreated from the biblical values and principles it was founded on. As our culture drifts further and further into secularism and hedonism and postmodernism, Christians are increasingly confronted with a choice: Should we speak out, loudly and clearly, for godliness and biblical truth in this dying culture? If we do, we may find ourselves challenging—and even abandoning—our former political allegiances and alliances.

When we take an unflinching look at the corruption of our leaders, we have to ask ourselves—why does the church have so little influence over our government? Why are we forced to choose a lesser evil instead of the greater good?

Why isn't the church raising up vast numbers of godly leaders to serve in our city councils, statehouses, and in Washington, DC?

If we lived under the oppression of a dictatorship or a monarchy, the church might have a good reason for having little impact on the government. But we live under a democratically elected representative government. Our national character should strongly reflect the character and influence of the church. And here is a troubling thought: *perhaps it does*.

What if the corruption in our government is merely a reflection of the corruption in the church? What if the abysmal candidates we are offered on election day are God's judgment against our country and against the apostasy of the church? One of the most frightening principles in Scripture is found in both the Old and New Testaments, in the recurring phrase "[God] gave them over." God, speaking through the Psalmist, said, "But my people would not listen to me; Israel would not submit to me. So I gave them over to their stubborn hearts to follow their own devices" (Psalm 81:11–12).

The martyr Stephen, in his speech to the Jewish ruling council before he was stoned to death, spoke God's response to Israel after the people made a golden calf and worshipped it in the desert: "But God turned away from them and gave them over to the worship of the sun, moon and stars" (Acts 7:42).

The apostle Paul, in his letter to the Romans, wrote about the ungodly people of the world, saying, "God gave them over in the sinful desires of their hearts" (Romans 1:24). There are numerous other Scripture passages describing this concept that I could cite. In each case, we see this principle at work: When people persist in their sin, God eventually removes His hand of protection from them and allows the consequences of sin to take their natural course.

So, if we in the church do not live out godliness in our own lives and if we do not demand godliness from our leaders, then we will get the leaders we deserve. We will get the government we deserve. God will give us over to the consequences of our own ungodliness.

"A LACK OF GREAT STATESMEN"

In Nazi Germany, the German state church became a willing accomplice of the Nazi Party. A minority movement of German Christians formed what they called "the Confessing Church," led by people of conscience, such as theologian Dietrich Bonhoeffer and youth evangelist Wilhelm Busch. The Confessing Church challenged and confronted Hitler and the Nazis. They tried to warn their fellow German churchmen that God would judge Christians who supported the godless Nazi regime.

Writing from prison, awaiting execution for opposing the Nazis, Bonhoeffer wrote, "One may ask whether there have ever before in human history been people with so little ground under their feet—people to whom every available alternative seemed equally intolerable, repugnant, and futile."[3]

When our American political system coughs up only candidates who seem "intolerable, repugnant, and futile," we should ask ourselves if God is trying to get our attention—or worse, if He has already handed us over to the consequences of our ungodliness.

On June 8, 1978, Aleksandr Solzhenitsyn, a Russian dissident, gave the commencement address at Harvard University. Solzhenitsyn had suffered greatly at the hands of the Soviet government, and he worried about the direction Western governments were taking. Speaking prophetically, he said, "There are meaningful warnings that history gives a threatened or perishing society. They are, for instance, the decadence of art, or a lack of great statesmen."[4]

It's clear that we are witnessing what Solzhenitsyn foretold—a "lack of great statesmen," signaling a warning that our civilization is threatened or already perishing. Solzhenitsyn, a devout Christian, was warning us that these cultural and political symptoms are warnings of God's impending judgment.

WHAT MAKES AMERICA EXCEPTIONAL?

Some Christians are under the mistaken impression that it is unpatriotic to criticize our government and our leaders. In reality, holding our country's leaders accountable is one of the great responsibilities we have, both as citizens and as Christians. Demanding honesty and integrity from our governmental leaders is one of the most patriotic things we can do.

We need to understand what we really mean when we say *America*. We need to understand that America is not the American government. America is not the American people. America is not a piece of real estate bordered by Canada to the north and Mexico to the south. America is a set of ideals and principles, embodied by its founding documents, the Declaration of Independence and the United States Constitution.

Most of us have heard of an idea called "American exceptionalism." What do people mean when they say that America is "exceptional"? Is America exceptional because of its great wealth and military might? No, that's not what makes this nation exceptional. Is America exceptional because its people have always behaved righteously? No—we have to confess that America's legacy of slavery, the mistreatment of Native Americans, and the injustices of the segregation era prove that America is as prone to wickedness, bigotry, and moral blindness as any other culture.

What, then, makes America exceptional? The answer is: American ideals. The principles embodied in the American founding documents are as flawless and righteous as any governing principles could be. "We hold these truths to be self-evident," asserts the Declaration of Independence, "that all men are created equal, that they are endowed by their Creator with certain unalienable Rights, that among these are Life, Liberty and the pursuit of Happiness.—That to secure these rights, Governments are instituted among Men, deriving their just powers from the consent of the governed."

"We the People of the United States," declares the Constitution, "in Order to form a more perfect Union, establish Justice, insure domestic Tranquility, provide for the common defense, promote the general Welfare, and secure the Blessings of Liberty to ourselves and our Posterity, do ordain and establish this Constitution for the United States of America."

And the First Amendment to that Constitution, the first pledge of the Bill of Rights, reads, "Congress shall make no law respecting an establishment of religion, or prohibiting the free exercise thereof; or abridging the freedom of speech, or of the press; or the right of the people peaceably to assemble, and to petition the Government for a redress of grievances."

These are exceptional principles, exceptional guarantees, exceptional declarations. They create a form of government that is unlike any government anywhere else in the world. When we say that America is exceptional, it's not a statement of pride or arrogance. It's a statement of humility and awe that God would bring together a group of fallible men and lead them through a contentious process of arguing and compromising, to produce these amazing documents.

Some of those who signed the statement that "all men are created equal" were, in fact, slave owners. There was a huge blind spot in their thinking. Yet the words they ratified rang in the conscience of a nation. Finally, on June 16, 1858, a man rose up and declared, in a speech before a thousand delegates in the statehouse in Springfield, Illinois, "'A house divided against itself cannot stand.' I believe this government cannot endure, permanently, half slave and half free. I do not expect the Union to be dissolved—I do not expect the house to fall—but I do expect it will cease to be divided. It will become all one thing or all the other." Those are the prophetic words of Abraham Lincoln.

The founding documents—the Declaration, the Constitution, the Bill of Rights, and the commentary on those documents, the Federalist Papers—seem almost divinely inspired. And in a sense, they are. Why? Because they were directly influenced by the principles of God's Word, both the Old and New Testaments. For example, it is commonly understood that the three branches of our government were inspired by Isaiah 33:22, which tells us that the Lord is our judge (judicial branch), our lawgiver (legislative branch), and our king (executive branch).

In those documents, We the People declared that our Creator is the source of our rights and liberties. We the

People rejected the dictatorship of a king across the water. We the People established a government of limited authority, in which our leaders are bound by the law and the Constitution, and accountable to the people. We the People have a right to openly criticize those in power, and even to remove them from office when they abuse their power.

And We the People have a right to practice our religious faith and obey our own conscience, without being accountable to, or censured by, the government.

WHAT BELONGS TO CAESAR, AND WHAT BELONGS TO GOD

Some time ago, I felt compelled as an American citizen and a minister of the gospel to criticize the actions of the president of the United States. After considerable prayer and soul-searching, I became convinced that the president's actions were a violation of the Constitution and of God's moral law. So I spoke out from the pulpit.

I received letters from Christians who took me to task, saying, "Don't you know that the Bible says we must honor the president and obey what he says?" They cited such Scripture passages as Romans 13:1–7 and 1 Peter 2:13–17. We need to always remember that Scripture interprets Scripture, and the passages that require us to obey the law and honor the king need to be weighed against those passages that require us to oppose unrighteous actions of the government. The same

Bible that says, "Let everyone be subject to the governing authorities" (Romans 13:1) also says, "We must obey God rather than human beings!" (Acts 5:29).

And there is another principle we need to understand as Christians in America—not a biblical principle but a constitutional principle. In America, the ultimate legal authority is not an emperor. The ultimate authority is the Constitution. In the United States, all public servants, from the highest to the lowest, take an oath to protect not a person but a document—the Constitution. The wording of the oath of office for the president of the United States is specified in Article 2, Section 1, Clause 8 of the Constitution: "I do solemnly swear (or affirm) that I will faithfully execute the Office of President of the United States, and will to the best of my Ability, preserve, protect and defend the Constitution of the United States."

The military oath of enlistment begins with similar wording: "I do solemnly swear (or affirm) that I will support and defend the Constitution of the United States against all enemies, foreign and domestic; that I will bear true faith and allegiance to the same."

Our civil allegiance is to the Constitution, not to a person. So when anyone in the government, up to and including the president, violates the Constitution, We the People have a right and an obligation to confront and disobey the government.

Our government officials regularly violate their oath and disobey the Constitution—and we as Americans and as Christians have a solemn responsibility to call them on it. One of the most blatant examples is the Johnson Amendment, a 1954 law that muzzles churches and gives the IRS the power to dictate what ministers of the gospel can preach from their pulpits. This is clearly a violation of two key provisions of the First Amendment—free speech and freedom of religion.

The Johnson Amendment was proposed by then senator Lyndon B. Johnson, who was angered over criticism he received from conservative preachers. By giving the IRS the power to take away the tax-exempt status of churches that spoke out on political issues and candidates, Senator Johnson silenced his opponents.

Christian commentator Cal Thomas has called the Johnson Amendment "the Berlin wall between church and state."[5] The government has no business telling ministers what they can and cannot preach about, whether the subject is salvation, abortion, or the corrupt behavior of politicians. God's Word has authority over every sphere of human activity, including the political sphere, and it is government that must be accountable to God, not the other way around.

Another unconstitutional action by our government, which I have spoken out against from the pulpit, is a joint statement released by the US Department of Justice and the US Department of Education on May 13, 2016. This statement was released a few days after the Justice Department filed suit against the state of North Carolina over a state law prohibiting people of the opposite sex from using public facilities.

The joint order requires every public school in America to allow any student claiming to be transgender (that is, having a self-identity not consistent with his or her physical sex) to use whichever restroom or locker room he or she chooses to use. According to that statement, school officials must not question that person's claim, must not require a medical or psychological diagnosis or documentation, and must accept that person's claim at face value.[6]

Though this joint letter from the US Departments of Education and Justice is technically nonbinding, states and school districts that fail to comply could lose millions in federal funding. Though this order is intended to respect the "feelings" of the tiny percentage of people who call themselves "transgender," it violates the constitutional rights and the feelings of the vast majority of people. No one— and especially not schoolchildren—should be forced to share restroom and locker room facilities with people of the opposite sex.

"Transgender rights" laws provide cover for voyeurs and predators—almost entirely men—who want to prey on women and girls. These laws give them the unquestioned right to enter any women's restroom or locker room. Anyone asking them to leave would risk a crippling lawsuit. There are already cases on record of men claiming to be transgendered women who have used these laws to commit lewd acts and secretly record their victims.

And there's a larger issue at stake: This order is a clear violation of the Tenth Amendment, which reads, "The powers not delegated to the United States by the Constitution, nor prohibited by it to the States, are reserved to the States respectively, or to the people." The federal government does not have the constitutional right to tell the states and the people how to regulate their restrooms. That right is reserved to the states and to the people.

The wording of the Tenth Amendment is absolutely clear. The president, the legislators, and justices of our courts all take an oath to protect and defend the Constitution— yet they regularly violate that oath. We the People have a duty to hold our leaders' feet to the fire whenever those feet trample on any portion of the Constitution. That is our right as citizens. That is our obligation as Christians.

It's important to always put principle ahead of party affiliation. We should treat our leaders with the same respect— and demand the same accountability—whether we voted for them or not, and whether they are members of our own party or the opposition party. In April 2016, when my state's

Republican governor vetoed the Georgia Religious Liberty Bill (HB 757), I spoke out from the pulpit. And when Atlanta's Democratic mayor unjustly fired Atlanta fire chief Kelvin J. Cochran, I again spoke out from the pulpit. It's principle, not party, that matters.

Chief Cochran was fired because he wrote a book about a biblical view of sexuality. I have read the book, and it proclaims the orthodox Protestant view of sexuality. Before he published the book, Chief Cochran asked for advice from the city's top ethics officer, who told him that as long as the book did not make any reference to city government or the fire department, he was free to write it.

Here is a man who hired many firefighters, reopened fire stations, reformed Atlanta's fire-rescue doctrine, and enabled Atlanta to achieve (for the first time ever) a Class I fire-protection rating (which only sixty American cities out of more than forty-nine thousand have earned). He has never been accused of discriminating in his hiring practices. Yet the mayor fired him for writing a Christian book. The mayor's actions violate the Constitution, and we as believers need to speak out against all injustice of this kind—not out of disrespect toward the mayor but out of respect for the Constitution.

Regardless of party affiliation, we must love and pray for our leaders, and always wish them well. But we cannot be silent when they abuse their power and their office. Jesus said that we are to "give back to Caesar what is Caesar's, and to God what is God's" (Matthew 22:21). In other words, we are to obey our governmental leaders and pay our taxes as responsible citizens—but whenever Caesar's laws are in conflict with God's law, we must obey God before Caesar.

The Word of God is neither Republican nor Democratic nor Libertarian nor Green. The Word of God has authority over all kingdoms, nations, and political affiliations.

11

THE HOPE FOR A NEW REFORMATION

CHIUNE SUGIHARA WAS BORN in 1900 in Japan. His father wanted him to go to medical school, but Chiune deliberately failed his entrance exams so he could attend Waseda University and study English. He received Jesus as his Lord and Savior at an early age, and while at the university, he joined a Japanese Christian fraternity, Yuai Gakusha.

After mastering English, Chiune studied Russian and German. His proficiency in languages enabled him to work in the Ministry of Foreign Affairs of Japan. While in his early twenties, he joined the Russian Orthodox Church and was baptized Pavlo Sergeivich Sugihara. The two Russian Christian names he took mean "Paul" and "Shepherd/ Protector."

During his early years in the Ministry of Foreign Affairs, Chiune was stationed in Manchuria, a region of northern China under Japanese control. There he witnessed Japanese government officials brutally oppressing the Manchurians. Conscience-stricken over the abuses he had witnessed, Chiune resigned his post in protest.

In 1939, the Japanese government posted him at the Japanese consulate in Kaunas, Lithuania. In December of that year, a Lithuanian Jewish boy invited Chiune and his wife to a Hanukkah celebration. Another Hanukkah guest was a Jewish man who had just escaped from Poland. Through tears, the man told Chiune that his wife and children had been killed by the Nazi invasion and bombing raids.

Chiune knew that Hitler's war was coming to Lithuania, and he was determined to help Lithuanian Jews escape by way of Japan. He asked his government for permission to issue transit visas so the Jews could escape to Japan. The Japanese government refused. So Chiune prayed for wisdom—then he told his wife, "I may have to disobey my government, but if I do not, I will be disobeying God. I know I should follow my conscience." His wife agreed.

On July 31, 1940, Chiune put his plan into action. He began writing transit visas by hand at a rate of three hundred per day. He worked long hours, taking quick meals at his desk, writing as rapidly as he could. As word spread,

Lithuanian Jews flocked to the consulate, pleading for visas.

On September 4, the Japanese government closed the consulate and ordered Chiune back to Japan. The night before he was to leave, he stayed up all night, writing visas. The next morning, he and his family boarded the train. A crowd of Lithuanian Jews surrounded the train. He handed out the visas he had written, saying, "Please forgive me. I cannot write any more." But once on the train, he kept writing more visas and tossing them out the window.

No one knows how many people were saved by Chiune Sugihara's act of obedience to God—and disobedience to his government. Estimates range from six thousand to ten thousand people.[1]

In 1985, the government of Israel awarded Chiune Sugihara its highest honor, naming him "Righteous among the Gentiles" for disobeying his government and saving so many Jewish lives. The following year, Chiune was called home by the Lord, where he received an even higher honor: "Well done, good and faithful servant" (Matthew 25:21, 23). Chiune Sugihara was a man who obeyed God's truth by disobeying his government.

As Chiune's story shows us, there are times when obedience to God demands disobedience to the government. Righteous civil disobedience is the only disobedience that God approves.

THE DISOBEDIENCE GOD APPROVES

I am grateful for the example of Dr. Martin Luther King Jr., who taught us how true biblical civil disobedience should be done. He never crossed the ethical line. He never used ungodly methods. He always stood firmly for justice and God's truth. Even though he was felled by an assassin's bullet, he achieved his goal of ending segregation in America.

Dr. King was inspired by a number of Christian writers, including Paul Tillich and Reinhold Niebuhr, and Russian novelist Leo Tolstoy. Dr. King was a key figure in the Montgomery Bus Boycott, which began in December 1955 when Rosa Parks refused to surrender her bus seat to a white passenger. Dr. King's house was fire-bombed during the boycott, but he continued to preach love as the best weapon against hate.

In his last speech, "I've Been to the Mountaintop," delivered April 3, 1968, in Memphis, Tennessee, Dr. King said:

> I don't know what will happen now. We've got some difficult days ahead. But it really doesn't matter with me now, because I've been to the mountaintop. And I don't mind.
>
> Like anybody, I would like to live a long life. Longevity has its place. But I'm not concerned about that now. I just want to do God's will. And He's allowed me to go up to the mountain. And I've looked

over. And I've seen the Promised Land. I may not get there with you. But I want you to know tonight, that we, as a people, will get to the Promised Land!

And so I'm happy tonight. I'm not worried about anything. I'm not fearing any man. Mine eyes have seen the glory of the coming of the Lord![2]

The following evening, at about six o'clock, Dr. King was assassinated as he stood on the balcony of his hotel room. There is often a price to pay for following the example of our Lord.

Some people claim that churches should never speak out about political issues because of "separation of church and state." Now, there's not one line in the Constitution about "separation of church and state." So where did that phrase come from?

President Thomas Jefferson coined the phrase "separation of church and state" in an 1802 letter to the Danbury Baptist Association of Connecticut. The Danbury Baptists were concerned that they might lose their freedom of religion, concerned that the government might one day try to regulate, limit, or in some way interfere with their religious expression. Jefferson wrote, "I contemplate with sovereign reverence that act of the whole American people which declared that their legislature should 'make no law respecting an establishment of religion, or prohibiting the free exercise thereof,' thus building a wall of separation between Church & State."[3]

The "wall of separation" President Jefferson referred to was never designed to prevent the church from influencing the government. Instead, it was intended to prevent the government from oppressing and silencing the church. Jefferson would be saddened (and probably infuriated) to see our constitutional *guarantee* of religious freedom used to *deny* religious freedom.

Like John Knox and Dr. Martin Luther King Jr., we must boldly declare that the state has no right to muzzle the church. In fact, one of the chief roles of the church is to hold the state accountable to God. The church wields the power of God's truth—and God's truth is much more powerful than man's sword.

RIGHTEOUS CIVIL DISOBEDIENCE

When the government violates any provision of the Constitution, we have a constitutional right *and a biblical responsibility* to speak out against those abuses and even to disobey the civil authorities. We see this principle again and again in the Scriptures.

When Pharaoh commanded two Hebrew midwives to kill male Hebrew babies, the midwives "feared God and did not do what the king of Egypt had told them to do; they let the boys live" (Exodus 1:17).

When the king of Jericho told Rahab the harlot to turn over the Hebrew spies, she refused—and she was commended in Scripture for her civil disobedience (Joshua 2; Hebrews 11:31).

King Saul once ordered that his own son Jonathan be put to death, but the soldiers refused the king's order and spared Jonathan (1 Samuel 14:45).

In 1 Kings 18, a man named Obadiah, a palace administrator who was a devout believer in the Lord, hid a hundred of God's prophets from the ungodly wrath of King Ahab and Queen Jezebel.

Peter and John, in the book of Acts, disobeyed both the corrupt religious authorities and the civil authorities who ordered them to stop preaching the gospel of Jesus Christ. Threatened with violence and imprisonment, Peter and John refused to back down. They declared, "We must obey God rather than human beings!" (Acts 5:29).

The Scriptures are absolutely clear: We are commanded by God to obey the law and honor the civil authorities—unless and until those laws and authorities come into conflict with God's law and God's authority. There is a clear hierarchy of authority, and God's authority is supreme over all others.

INTEGRITY IN THE SMALL THINGS

The Bible gives us many examples of how God's people, who belong to the City of God, can stand firm against the hostility and injustice of the City of Man. A prime example is the prophet Daniel and his three friends, Shadrach, Meshach, and Abednego.

Civil disobedience is a key theme of the book of Daniel. In Daniel 3, Shadrach, Meshach, and Abednego refuse to comply with King Nebuchadnezzar's order to bow down to and worship his golden image. And in Daniel 6, Daniel defies the decree of King Darius requiring that prayers be made only to the king.

These four men belonged to the City of God—yet they were captives of the ultimate City of Man, Babylon itself. They faced tremendous pressure to conform. The government told them to obey—or die. The government told them that the king's authority was final. The government told them to keep their mouths shut. The government told them to keep their religion to themselves. And the government told them to worship their narcissistic king.

Obey or die—that was the stark choice Daniel and his companions faced. Yet they believed that God was in control of history, and they refused to bow the knee to the idol of the king. So Daniel and his three friends were accused of crimes against the state. They were blamed for the ills of society, just as Christians are often blamed today. For a while, it appeared that God's enemies had all the power and control.

Yet Daniel and his friends refused to surrender. They continued to trust God. They were called intolerant because they refused to approve and participate in evil and idolatry. Their captors gave them new, Babylonian names, hoping to convert them to the worship of the false Babylonian gods. But Daniel and his three friends—who were only teenagers at the time—refused to compromise. They might have pagan names, but they would continue to serve the one true God.

Not all of the issues Daniel and his friends faced were as obvious as blatant idolatry. Some of the pressures they faced from the Babylonian government were subtler. For example, in Daniel 1:8 we read, "But Daniel resolved not to defile himself with the royal food and wine, and he asked the chief official for permission not to defile himself this way." In other words, after considerable time in prayer and seeking God's will, Daniel decided that God did not want him to defile himself with Babylon's "royal junk food."

Daniel could have said to himself, "I want to live for God in all the *big* issues. No idolatry for me! But why make a fuss over a petty little issue like food? The Babylonians eat this royal junk food, and they seem healthy enough. On the small matters, I'm going to go along to get along."

But here's the principle that Daniel lived by: Great victories are often won in small matters. If we maintain our integrity in the little things, then the big things will take care of themselves. If we never steal so much as a paper clip from the office, then we'll never get caught embezzling a million dollars. If we refuse to tell even little white lies, then we'll never go to prison for perjury. Because Daniel refused to compromise his integrity and faithful obedience to God on the smallest issues, he was prepared to stand his ground on the big issues as well.

THE CROSS OF JESUS CHRIST

These days, one of the issues many churches have begun compromising is the cross of Jesus Christ. One such church was Christ Community Church in Spring Lake, Michigan, which changed its name to C3Exchange. When the church removed the forty-foot-tall steel cross and the name of Christ from the building, the minister explained, "Our community has been a really open-minded community for some years now. We've had a number of Muslim people, Jewish people, Buddhists, atheists. . . . The cross has become a negative symbol for a lot of people."[4]

To all who understand its meaning, the cross of Jesus Christ is the greatest symbol of love the world has ever known. The banishment of that cross from so many churches demonstrates a lack of understanding of what the cross means to those who belong to the City of God. Where there is no cross, there is no good news being preached. As the pulpit goes, so goes the pew. And as the pew goes, so goes the civilization.

One of the ironies of this story is that, as often happens when a church seeks friendship with the world, it begins to die. After removing the cross and changing its name to C3Exchange, the church struggled to meet its mortgage payments. The church moved out and began holding services at a local community center.[5]

Believers from another church in town, Harvest Bible Chapel, valued that cross. They didn't want to see that gleaming symbol of the Lord's sacrifice end up on a scrap heap. So Harvest Bible Chapel moved into the property and reinstalled the cross in time for the Good Friday 2013 service.

The removal of a cross may seem to be a small matter. But we have to ask ourselves—why are so many people in our culture, and in the church, offended by the cross? At its very core, the reason people in our Western civilization hate the cross is the same ultimate reason that the barbarian terrorists hate the cross: This is a spiritual battle. There are powerful spiritual, evil forces that want to suppress the cross of Jesus Christ because it is God's only answer to sin.

We must always raise the cross high—not in a spirit of self-righteousness, but in a spirit of humility. We have no power to save ourselves—we are saved by the cross of Christ alone.

The City of Man is hostile to us and hostile to our gospel. That's why Jesus says that we need to love our enemies, do good to those who hate us, bless those who curse us, and pray for those who mistreat us (Luke 6:27–28). We must always speak the truth in love (Ephesians 4:15). Above all, we lift high the cross of Jesus Christ, because—as the apostle Paul reminds us—"the message of the cross is foolishness to those who are perishing, but to us who are being saved it is the power of God" (1 Corinthians 1:18).

Lift high the cross, my beloved friend. Lift high the cross!

TIME FOR A NEW REFORMATION

Western civilization is the product of the Reformation. The Reformers threw open the windows of God's light after a thousand years of spiritual and cultural darkness. Today, as the barbarians are again infiltrating our civilization, as the church drifts into error, ignorance, and apostasy, the time has come for a New Reformation.

What would that New Reformation look like?

It would call men and women in the church to repent of all the things they have added to the gospel—or have taken away from the gospel. It would call them to preach God's truth out of pure motives, instead of from a lust for wealth or fame. It would call them to put away the false teaching and idols of the Prosperity Gospel, the Social Gospel, the Emerging Church, and all the other distortions and perversions of the good news of Jesus Christ.

A New Reformation would expose the lies that have blinded so many professing Christians in our time. A New Reformation would awaken our Western civilization from the false hope that we can bargain with the barbarians or persuade them to turn from their way of destruction. A New Reformation would be rooted in realism, not wishful thinking, and it would recognize that those who seek to destroy our civilization and our faith will never abandon their quest. Only the good news of Jesus Christ can melt a barbarian heart.

A New Reformation would stand in opposition not only to political Islam but would also stand in opposition to the City of Man—our secular Western society, drunk on wealth, power, sexual immorality, and drugs. Much of the Islamists' hatred of Western civilization is rooted in a mistaken belief that all of the ills of secular society are somehow caused and condoned by the church.

A New Reformation would draw a clear distinction between the City of God and the City of Man. A New Reformation would show the world the face of authentic biblical Christianity—a Christianity that preaches the good news of Jesus Christ without compromise, that demonstrates truth and love in perfect balance, and that cares about people in need but refuses to back down from the truth in the face of threats and terrorism.

A New Reformation is the only hope Western civilization has to reverse its present course of destruction. The God of the New Reformation is the God of mercy and grace. He is the God who hung on a cross to redeem humanity, the God who rose again to prove His divine power.

Today, with arms open wide, the Lord Jesus calls to the world, to all people of East and West, to everyone living in the City of Man, "Repent and come to Me. Come live forever in the City of God. This world is heading for destruction, but I have made a way of escape for you—a way of salvation."

Come, Lord Jesus!

12

FINDING OUR WAY HOME

THAHIR SAHAB JAMEL was a Sunni Arab in his early twenties, living with his mother and three brothers in the village of Hawija in northern Iraq. He made a decent living, working on a farm. He had been a teenager in 2003 when American-led forces invaded Iraq and toppled Saddam Hussein. During the American occupation, the country had remained unstable and torn by conflict and terror attacks. After the American withdrawal in 2011, violence and unrest surged throughout the country.

But Thahir Jamel was concerned only with keeping his job and providing for his mother and brothers. He didn't care about politics.

One day a stranger named Salam came to visit him. The man spoke with intensity and passion about the Sunni

Muslim religion. "You must join the struggle," Salam said. "You must become a [jihadist] and help bring down the Shia government. We're going to raise up the caliphate and fulfill the ancient prophecies."

Jamel found Salam's recruitment speech appealing. This man was calling him out of his humdrum existence and into a struggle that would give his life meaning and purpose. So he left his job and family, and he joined a movement that was practically unknown at the time but would soon become the world's most-feared army of terrorists—an army known as ISIS, the Islamic State in Iraq and Syria. He pledged his allegiance to the self-proclaimed caliph of the Islamic State, Abu Bakr al-Baghdadi.

He soon began training with other recruits in their early twenties. His trainers were battle-hardened soldiers in their forties and fifties—men who had served in Saddam Hussein's army, men of cunning, cruelty, and bloody experience. They talked about taking over the nation of Iraq, killing the "infidels" [non-Muslims] and evildoers, and establishing a caliphate ruled by Sharia law, based on the Quran. The caliphate would control the economy and would seize revenue from captured oilfields. The leaders talked about expanding the caliphate far beyond the borders of Syria and Iraq. They would retake Palestine and spread north into Europe, south into Africa, and east into Asia. Infidels would submit to the Islamic State—or be destroyed.

Jamel rose in the ranks, becoming an *emir* (a lord or commander), with a level of responsibility roughly equivalent to a captain in the army. He was placed in charge of a company of seventy fighters. His mission was to carry out brutal attacks in the battle-scarred, oil-rich region around Baiji, on the road between Baghdad and Mosul. Jamel's ISIS forces rolled up a string of impressive victories, helping to spread the caliphate across northern Iraq.

For a year and a half, Jamel and his company of terrorists waged war against civilians and soldiers, slaughtering "infidel" men, women, and children without the slightest pang of conscience. He and his men took part in public beheadings and other grisly executions of civilians in order to keep the populations in the villages in submission. He turned over many civilians to his ISIS superiors, knowing they faced the most horrifying tortures imaginable, followed by brutal execution. He carried out the orders of the Islamic State without question. Some of those orders were issued by Caliph Abu Bakr al-Baghdadi himself.

In May 2016, Jamel and some of his men were arrested by government police in a village near the northern city of Kirkuk. As I write these words, Thahir Sahab Jamel awaits trial for his crimes. He may receive life in prison—or death by hanging.

Handcuffed, his face covered by a mask, Jamel gave an interview to an American news agency. He claims he now regrets his crimes. "It haunts me that I am responsible for killing many people," he says. "We killed them for nothing."

The head of the police force that captured Jamel says that all captured ISIS fighters express regret, but there's no way to know if they are sincere or not. They all seem to develop a conscience the moment they are arrested.

Thahir Jamel once believed he would die a martyr's death, but now he fears eternal damnation. "At the beginning, ISIS told us we would all go to heaven," he said. "Now that I am in prison it means I am going to the fire. I am going to hell."[1]

My heart breaks for this man's victims—but my heart also breaks for Jamel himself. He was so deceived by the false ideology of political Islam that he left his job and family to become a soldier of the caliphate. Thahir Sahab Jamel is just one young man among thousands who have been lured into the death cult of ISIS. Promised heaven, he became a soldier of hell. Made an emir of the Islamic State, he became a barbarian.

As we have seen, there are many more barbarians where he came from. They are coming. In fact, thousands are already here.

Remember, as I explained in chapter 1, I am not using the term *barbarian* as an exercise in name-calling or insults. I have chosen this word carefully because it has a specific meaning. A barbarian is a person who is not part of our civilization, who wants no part of our civilization, and who seeks the conquest and destruction of our civilization, just as the Visigoths sacked the city of Rome.

I don't blame the barbarians for doing what barbarians do. I hold the church responsible for not doing what the church was established by God to do. And I believe God will hold the church accountable for failing to be the church, and for peddling an adulterated and false "gospel."

From the time our first parents, Adam and Eve, chose to go their own way instead of God's way, human beings have reaped the consequences of their rebellion: they were exiled from the Garden. When Israel chose spiritual adultery over faithfulness to God, the consequences were the same: they were exiled from the land God gave them.

Today, as the church chooses to go its own way instead of lifting up the pure, unadulterated gospel of Jesus Christ, we are facing a different kind of exile that is coming our way—terrorism. Our secular political leaders, in their greed and ignorance, have invited the barbarians into the City of Man.

If God's hand of protection has been removed from us, it's because we in the church, in our disobedience to God, have left the gates of the City unlocked.

HOPE FOR CIVILIZATION

There is a way back to God. There is a pathway to blessing for the church and for our culture. It's the pathway of God's truth. It requires us to turn away from the spiritual and moral relativism that pervades our culture. It demands that we be faithful to the pure and simple truth of the Christian gospel.

Even during the Babylonian Exile, there was a faithful remnant. There was a small but committed nucleus of believers who refused to compromise God's truth.

When the government of King Nebuchadnezzar ordered all of the people—both the Babylonians and the captive Hebrews—to worship the king's image, almost everyone obeyed. But a faithful few—Shadrach, Meshach, and Abednego—refused the order, preferring the fiery furnace over sin.

And when King Darius of Persia ordered that no prayers be offered to any god or person except himself, Daniel remained faithful to God and dared to refuse the order. The king sent Daniel to the lions' den, but God blessed Daniel and shut the mouths of the lions—and God blessed Israel because of Daniel's faithfulness.

Just as there has always been a faithful remnant in Israel, even while the nation was in exile, so there is a faithful remnant in the church today. Those godly believers are daily on their knees, praying that God would restore the church and heal the nation. They speak out, they fast and pray, and they tell others the good news, even as the world is collapsing all around them.

God has commanded us to live faithfully and pray earnestly for the welfare of the city of our exile—in our case, the

City of Man, Western civilization. Jeremiah wrote, "Seek the peace and prosperity of the city to which I have carried you into exile. Pray to the LORD for it, because if it prospers, you too will prosper" (Jeremiah 29:7). Even though the City of Man is secularized and ungodly, it is our temporary home while we await our eternal home, the City of God, the New Jerusalem. If we bless the City of Man by our faithfulness to God and by our witness for Him, then we will trigger a hunger in the people around us for the good news.

THE PURE GOSPEL

After we clear away all the falsehood, error, and ignorance of the Emerging Church, the Prosperity Gospel, the Social Gospel, and all the other counterfeit "gospels" of our time, what is the absolute truth that remains? Jesus Himself gave the simplest formulation of the gospel when He told the Pharisee Nicodemus, "For God so loved the world that he gave his one and only Son, that whoever believes in him shall not perish but have eternal life" (John 3:16).

The apostle Paul also gave a simple four-part outline of the gospel in his first letter to the church at Corinth. I have indicated each of those four parts with a bracketed number in bold type:

> Now, brothers and sisters, I want to remind you of the
> gospel I preached to you, which you received and on

which you have taken your stand. By this gospel you are saved, if you hold firmly to the word I preached to you. Otherwise, you have believed in vain.

For what I received I passed on to you as of first importance: **[1]** that Christ died for our sins according to the Scriptures, **[2]** that he was buried, **[3]** that he was raised on the third day according to the Scriptures, and **[4]** that he appeared to Cephas, and then to the Twelve. After that, he appeared to more than five hundred of the brothers and sisters at the same time, most of whom are still living, though some have fallen asleep. Then he appeared to James, then to all the apostles, and last of all he appeared to me also, as to one abnormally born. (1 Corinthians 15:1–8)

Let's look at each of those four parts of the gospel:

Part 1: Jesus died for our sins.
Part 2: Jesus was buried.
Part 3: Jesus rose again on the third day.
Part 4: The resurrection of the Lord Jesus was verified by many witnesses.

Paul tells us that this is the gospel message in a nutshell. This is the essence of the good news.

A number of essential truths are implied in those four parts of the gospel. For example, the reason Christ died for our sins is that *we are sinners and incapable of saving ourselves.* And the reason Paul twice says "according to the Scriptures" is because Old Testament prophecy stated clearly that God's Anointed One, the Messiah, would have to die, would have to be buried, and would be raised again—and those prophecies establish the Lord's credentials as the promised Messiah (see, for example, Psalm 16:10 and Isaiah 53:8–10).

The reason it's important that the resurrection of Jesus Christ was verified by witnesses is so that no one can justifiably say that the resurrection is a mere "narrative" or "comforting myth." The resurrection of the Lord Jesus is a historical fact. Anyone who denies any of four parts of the gospel—the Lord's death, His burial, His resurrection, or the verification of the resurrection by witnesses—denies the gospel and is a false teacher.

We must not subtract any of those four ingredients from the gospel. We must not add any unbiblical doctrines or practices to that gospel.

FOCUS ON JESUS CHRIST

In chapter 1, I described a number of movements that have sometimes replaced the purity of the gospel with the political notions of either the Religious Right or the Religious Left, or the economic and sociological theories of the Social Gospel, or the greed and distorted theology of the Prosperity Gospel, or the universalism and "post-evangelical deconstructionism" of the Emerging Church.

The biggest difference between all of these false "gospels" and the one true gospel of Jesus Christ is *who is the focus of each gospel*. In every false "gospel," the focus is on us, on our political views, on our well-being, on our view of the biblical narrative, on our observance of rites and rituals, on our own good works, on our own opinion of God's character, on our own emotional experiences, or on our own positive thinking. In the gospel of Jesus Christ, the focus is on Jesus— His death, His burial, His resurrection, the prophecies about Him, and the witnesses who verified His resurrection.

All false "gospels" are human-centered. The one true gospel is Christ-centered.

In the one true gospel, even the hope of heaven is focused not so much on us and our enjoyment of heaven, but on the fact that we will be in heaven *with Christ*. He is "the Alpha and the Omega, the Beginning and the End" (Revelation 21:6). And because Jesus is the First and the Last, and the focus of all creation, all the false religions of the world try to dethrone Him and remove Him from the picture.

No religion has done a better job of dethroning Jesus and inflicting spiritual blindness on its followers then the religion of Islam. Remember the attack on the Catholic priest in

Normandy in July 2016? The two Muslim teenagers slashed the throat of an eighty-five-year-old priest, then told a pair of horrified nuns, "Jesus cannot be God and a man." Barbarians like these would not hesitate to kill us for saying that Jesus is the Son of God.

The Christian gospel places the Lord Jesus at the center of everything. He is the focus of our hope of heaven. He is "the way and the truth and the life" (John 14:6). He is the reason we are not afraid to live—and not afraid to die.

We who know Jesus as our Lord and Savior belong to the City of God, even though we are sojourners in the City of Man. We are on earth as ambassadors of heaven. And an ambassador never forgets his home country. We have been sent to the City of Man to call others out of that city and to invite them into the City of God. We are here as witnesses to represent Jesus. We are here as salt to preserve society and keep it from corruption. We are placed here as light to illuminate society and point the way to God.

If you have never received Jesus as your Lord and Savior, I plead with you to flee the coming judgment. Flee the wrath of God by running into the loving arms of God. Flee eternal death by choosing eternal life. Receive the free gift of salvation that Jesus offers you by grace through faith in Him.

Look heavenward. Fix your eyes on the prize. And what is the heavenly prize? The City of God, the New Jerusalem.

WHY WE LOSE SIGHT OF HEAVEN

Why do so many believers lose sight of their eternal hope? Why do so many Christians take their eyes off the prize of their heavenly dwelling place, the City of God? I believe we lose sight of our eternal habitation for five reasons.

We Have a False Perception of Heaven

There are many distorted images of heaven in our culture, keeping us from desiring the wonderful heavenly city Jesus has prepared for us.

Ted Turner started the first twenty-four-hour cable news outlet, amassed a $10 billion fortune, and married a movie star—but he doesn't want to go to heaven. Why? Because he has a false perception of heaven. "I can't see myself sitting on a cloud and playing the harp day in and day out," he once said.[2] In spite of his vast wealth and accomplishments, I pity him.

Nowhere does the Bible tell us that heaven will involve sitting on a cloud, playing a harp for eternity. Or singing choruses. Or wearing halos over our heads. Or any of the other odd notions people have about heaven. The reality of the City of God is far beyond our ability to describe or imagine. That's why the Bible gives us only brief glimpses of the heavenly reality. If we could see heaven in its true splendor, believers would jump off of skyscrapers to get there.

Think of the most beautiful scene you've ever witnessed, combined with the most exalted feelings of wonder you've ever felt—then multiply that a billion times over, and you *might* begin to approach the reality of heaven. As Paul wrote, ". . . as it is written: 'What no eye has seen, what no ear has heard, and what no human mind has conceived'—the things God has prepared for those who love him" (1 Corinthians 2:9). Paul had a truer understanding of the wonders of heaven than almost anyone who has ever lived. That's why he wrote, "I am torn between the two: I desire to depart and be with Christ, which is better by far; but it is more necessary for you that I remain in the body" (Philippians 1:23–24).

False perceptions of the New Jerusalem will lead us to take our eyes off the prize. The more accurate our expectation of heaven, the more we will desire and seek it.

The Pressures of This Life Eclipse Our Vision of Heaven

The problems of our daily lives can steal our heavenly focus. When all we can see are the financial problems we must solve, the angry boss we must face, the family crises we must deal with, the emotional wear and tear we must endure, the suffering and death of our loved ones—all of these pressures eclipse our vision of heaven.

No, we mustn't neglect our responsibilities in order to stare heavenward. It's right that we shoulder our responsibilities, meet our obligations, and live faithfully as good stewards. It's right that we show compassion to loved ones and shepherd those who depend on us.

But all of the good and important things we do should be done with one purpose in mind: to serve the Lord and to attract others to the Savior. Let's use the pressures of this life to enlarge our witness for Jesus. As we face problems and pressures, let's do so with Christlike grace, perseverance, and love. May the light of God's character shine through us as we face our struggles and temptations.

My beloved friend, this world is desperate to know God and to find a realistic hope of heaven. This world hates us and mocks us—but God calls us to forgive and love our enemies with the love of Jesus. He calls us to bless when others curse us, and to do good to those who hurt us. When they breathe the curses of hell against us, we pray that God will draw them to heaven.

The pressures of this life can tempt us to take our eyes off the prize. But if we view this life through the eyes of Jesus, even our worst days will be illuminated with the light of heaven.

The Allure of This Life Blinds Us to the Unseen Reality of Heaven

Because of our nature, the things we see with our eyes get our attention. The visible world tugs at our thoughts and emotions. As the saying goes, "Out of sight, out of mind." So we spend little time thinking about the wondrous—but unseen—realities of heaven.

Our secularized culture tells us that "heaven" is just a fairy tale—a myth we tell ourselves because we can't face the finality of death. If we can't see heaven, or experience it with any of our other senses, then it must not be real.

As a result, many people today think that heaven is make-believe—and equally tragic, they think that make-believe is reality. People become so involved with their favorite TV shows, computer games, movies, or novels that fictional characters become more real to them than actual people.

I once heard of a soap opera in which one of the lead characters was killed off. No, the actor didn't die—just the fictional character. Fans of the soap opera were devastated. The production company was flooded with thousands of sympathy cards and floral bouquets. These fans were grief stricken at the "death" of a make-believe person. On some level, I think those grief-stricken fans must have been unable to distinguish fantasy from reality.

But far more tragic are those people who fail to recognize the reality of heaven. The Word of God is clear: If we want to live in heaven in eternity, then we must place our trust in the Lord Jesus Christ. If we want to invest in eternity, then we must risk everything on Him, knowing that only what we give to God will be waiting for us in heaven—and we will reap our reward with interest!

The Apostasy and Worldliness of the Church Muddles How We Think About Heaven

Go to any church, select a parishioner at random, and ask, "What are your spiritual goals in life? What are you doing to accomplish God's purpose for your existence on earth?" I think you may be shocked at the answers.

"Spiritual goals?" you might hear. "I'm not sure what you mean. I have financial goals. I have goals for my retirement. I have goals for traveling and playing a lot of golf. Is that what you mean?"

Christians in the early church had very simple goals. They lived and worked to glorify God and to spread the good news of Jesus Christ far and wide. They didn't plan for retirement. They planned for eternity.

The number one priority for most Christians today is *happiness*. For the early church, every believer's priority was *holiness*. Whereas the early church practiced self-sacrifice, the church today practices self-satisfaction. The early Christians risked all for Christ; Christians today try to eliminate all risk from their lives.

Early Christians glorified God. We gratify the self. Early Christians counted it a privilege to be martyred for Christ. We act like martyrs whenever we are mildly inconvenienced.

We need to recapture what it means to dare great things for God. We need to revive an old-fashioned zeal for the holiness of God. And we need to set spiritual goals for becoming more like Christ and for laying up treasures in heaven. Let's be less worldly and more otherworldly. Let's keep the vision of the New Jerusalem ever before us.

False Teaching Leaves Us Ignorant and Deceived About Heaven

Many pastors have quit teaching about heaven and hell. They focus on whatever themes are popular—successful living, improving your relationships, repairing your self-esteem, and other human-centered subjects.

We in the ministry have an obligation to major on what the Bible majors on, and the Bible has a lot to say about heaven and hell. If we refuse to talk about what the Bible *continually* talks about, we are not teaching the full counsel of God, and we are not being faithful to the authority of God's Word. And we're cheating those we've been called to shepherd.

Some ministers who call themselves "evangelicals" refuse to preach the good news. This is ironic because the word *evangelical* comes from the Greek word *evangelion*, which means "good news." Any minister who refuses to teach that the Lord Jesus Christ is "the way and the truth and the life" (John 14:6) should stop using the label "evangelical."

A number of years ago, I visited with a minister from a mainline denomination. I told him that I preached Jesus as the only way to God the Father. He actually found that message—the gospel message—infuriating. He looked at me with anger and frustration and said, "How arrogant of you to say that Jesus is the only way to heaven!"

I looked at him with sadness. "Your false teaching," I said, "misleads people all the way to hell. Your false teaching confuses even professing Christians. I didn't invent the idea that Jesus is the only way to God the Father. Jesus Himself said, 'No one comes to the Father but by me.' It would be arrogant for me to contradict what the Lord Himself has said."

I pleaded with this man and begged him to accept the claim that Jesus made about Himself—to no avail. Years ago, when I had that conversation, the teaching that there are many roads to God was rare even in mainline denominations. Today, such teaching is rampant. Apostasy and false teaching are everywhere, pervading even many so-called evangelical churches.

There can be little doubt that the spread of apostasy is preparing the world for a one-world religion and the rise of the Antichrist. Jesus said, "At that time many will turn away from the faith and will betray and hate each other, and many false prophets will appear and deceive many people" (Matthew 24:10–11). We are already seeing these signs come to pass.

The world is moving quickly toward the end times. You and I are called to say, as the writer to the Hebrews wrote, "For here we do not have an enduring city, but we are looking for the city that is to come" (Hebrews 13:14).

"YOU'RE NOT HOME YET"

I am a joy-filled Christian. I love my life as much as you love yours. I love serving the Lord in this life. I love serving God's people through the spoken and written word. I love my family, and I dearly enjoy spending time and blessed fellowship with them.

But I know I'm just a sojourner in this world. Every waking moment, I am looking forward to the City that is to come, the City of God. And my longing for that City grows more and more each day.

I once heard the story of Henry Clay Morrison, who was considered one of the great preachers and evangelists of the late nineteenth and early twentieth centuries. In 1910, he took a trip around the world by steamship. At every port the steamship docked, Dr. Morrison would organize evangelistic meetings and preach the gospel to thousands of people. According to his count, more than ten thousand people made decisions for Christ during that journey.

Dr. Morrison's trip took him from New York through the Panama Canal, across the Pacific, through the Indian Ocean, all the way to Africa. While docked in Africa, the ship picked up a world-famous passenger and his entourage. That passenger was none other than Theodore Roosevelt, the former president of the United States. Just days after leaving office in March 1909, President Roosevelt had set off on a yearlong African safari known as the Smithsonian-Roosevelt African Expedition—and now the former president was returning to the States.

The steamship crossed the Atlantic, and for Dr. Morrison it was a miserable voyage. The Roosevelt Expedition monopolized the ship, and there were sections of the ship that were off-limits to regular passengers like Dr. Morrison.

Finally, the ship pulled into New York Harbor. At the dock, the governor of New York and the mayor of New York City were on hand to greet the returning president. A band played and thousands of people thronged the wharf. Dr. Morrison watched as President Roosevelt stepped down the gangplank to thunderous applause. Then he stood on a platform and gave a speech, which received another ovation.

Years later, when he talked about this experience, Dr. Morrison admitted that he felt a bit envious and a bit sorry for himself. "Where had President Roosevelt been? What was he doing?" the evangelist asked himself. "He was over in Africa, shooting water hogs."

As Henry Clay Morrison stepped onto the wharf, there were no crowds, no brass bands, no dignitaries to greet him. No one waved flags for him; no one applauded; no whistles blew. Dr. Morrison didn't even have a friend or relative to greet him.

He picked up his heavy suitcases, walked alone to the train station, and bought his ticket for the trip to his hometown. He later recalled his thoughts as the train pulled out of the station and rumbled down the tracks. "I could not help but contrast the homecoming of Roosevelt with my own," he said. "God had privileged me to lead ten thousand souls to Christ on that trip—yet there I was, without a soul to meet me. Nobody welcomed me—nobody cared!"

Then a new thought occurred to him, a thought that seem to come from God Himself. And Dr. Morrison found himself saying aloud, "I know why no one was there to meet me. I'm not home yet! I'm not home!"[3]

And so it is with you and me. We spend our lives following Christ, serving Christ, preaching Christ, sharing Christ—and sometimes we wonder if it's worth it. No one seems to notice. No one seems to care. Other people seem to get all the acclaim, all the wealth, all the success—and what do we have to show for serving Christ?

We mustn't forget that we are still standing on the wharf in the City of Man. We shouldn't expect a welcoming committee and brass bands. We're still on our journey.

We're not home yet.

When we finally reach the New Jerusalem, then we'll be home. Then we'll be in the City of God forever. And when we arrive, we'll receive a greater welcome than we could ever imagine. The Lord Himself will be there—and He will acknowledge all our sacrifice, our labor, and our devotion.

And after a lifetime of serving Him, we'll finally hear the words we've been longing to hear: "Well done, good and faithful servant! . . . Come and share your master's happiness!" (Matthew 25:21, 23).

Keep believing. Keep serving. It won't be long.

Just wait till you get home!

NOTES

Chapter 1: Terrorism—Our Exile

1. Voice of the Martyrs, "Libya: 'Their God Is My God,'" Persecution.com, April 9, 2015, http://www.persecution.com/public/newsroom.aspx?story_ID=%3D373535; Jared Malsin, "ISIS Sets Sights on Europe in Latest Beheading Video," Time.com, February 16, 2015, http://time.com/3711022/isis-libya-copts/.

2. The White House, Office of the Press Secretary, "Statement by the Press Secretary on the Murder of Egyptian Citizens," February 15, 2015, https://www.whitehouse.gov /the-press-office/2015/02/15/statement-press-secretary-murder-egyptian-citizens.

3. Mufti A. H. Elias and Mohammad Ali ibn Zubair Ali, "Imam Mahdi (Descendent of Prophet Muhammad PBUH)," Islam.tc, accessed October 20, 2016, http://www.islam .tc/prophecies/imam.html.

4. Eurostat, "Asylum Statistics," data extracted on March 2, 2016 and April 20, 2016, page last modified May 11, 2016, http://ec.europa.eu/eurostat/statistics-explained /index.php/Asylum_statistics.

5. "Muslims Immigrants to Europe: 'May Allah Make Orphans out of Their Children' ALL SAYS AMEN" [*sic*], YouTube video, 0:45, footage taken on a refugee train, posted by MegaPhylum, September 10, 2015, https://www.youtube.com/watch?v =NQP4v2bm-hk.

6. Patrick Goodenough, "10,126: Administration Hits Syria Refugee Target; 0.5% Are Christians," CNS News, August 29, 2016, http://www.cnsnews.com/news/article /patrick-goodenough/10000-administration-about-hit-syria-refugee-target-fewer-05-are.

7. Jonathan Witt, "Why So Few Syrian Christian Refugees?," *Stream*, November 20, 2015, https://stream.org/why-so-few-syrian-christian-refugees/

8. Muhammad Sa'eed Al Qahtani, "Hijrah: Migration for the Cause of Allah," excerpt from *Al Wala' wa'l Bara*, Mission Islam, https://www.missionislam.com/knowledge /hijrah.htm.

9. Quilliam Foundation, "Quilliam Exclusive—Translation and Analysis of Islamic State Document Highlighting Its Strategic Goals in Libya," Quilliam, February 18, 2015, http://www.quilliamfoundation.org/press/quilliam-exclusive-translation-and-analysis -of-islamic-state-document-highlighting-its-strategic-goals-in-libya/; Charlie Winter, *Libya: The Strategic Gateway for the Islamic State: Translation and Analysis of IS Recruitment Propaganda for Libya*, Quilliam Foundation, February 2015, http://www .quilliamfoundation.org/wp/wp-content/uploads/publications/free/libya-the-strategic -gateway-for-the-is.pdf.

10. *Times of Israel* staff, "Breed and Conquer Europe, al-Aqsa Preacher Exhorts Muslims," *Times of Israel*, September 19, 2015, http://www.timesofisrael.com/breed-and-conquer -europe-al-aqsa-preacher-exhorts-muslims/; "Top Muslim Imam: Breed with Europeans to Conquer Them!," YouTube video, 2:39, posted by European American Vanguard, September 19, 2015, https://www.youtube.com/watch?v=Bgrc1QIDLOo.

11. Richard Fausset, "SUV Attack Prompts Debate over 'Terrorism' and Islam," *Los Angeles Times*, March 7, 2006, http://articles.latimes.com/2006/mar/07/nation/na -plow7.

12. First Community Church, "Exploring the Myths, Realities and Spiritual Practices of Islam: Fall 2015 Spiritual Searcher Speaker: Imam Feisal Abdul Rauf—October 2–4," FCCChurch.com, http://fcchurch.com/imam/.

13. Paula R. Kincaid, "Prayers to Allah Offered at PCUSA's General Assembly Plenary Session (Updated)," *The Layman* blog, June 22, 2016, http://www.layman.org/prayers -allah-offered-pcusas-general-assembly-plenary-session/.

14. Victor Davis Hanson, *Carnage and Culture: Landmark Battles in the Rise of Western Power* (New York: Anchor Books, 2001), 166.

15. Blake Neff, "Historicity and Holy War: Putting the Crusades in Context," *Dartmouth Apologia* 6, no. 1 (Fall 2011), Augustine Collective, http://augustinecollective.org /augustine/historicity-holy-war-putting-the-crusades-in-context.

16. Robert Louis Wilken, *The First Thousand Years: A Global History of Christianity* (New Haven: Yale University Press, 2012), 307, 308.

17. George Santayana, *The Life of Reason*, vol. 1, *Reason in Common Sense* (1905), http://www.gutenberg.org/files/15000/15000-h/vol1.html.

Chapter 2: Invasion of Other Gods

1. James Strong, *Strong's Concordance with Hebrew and Greek Lexicon (The Exhaustive Concordance of the Bible)*, "Lexicon: Strong's G572—*haplotēs*," https://www .blueletterbible.org/lang/Lexicon/Lexicon.cfm?strongs=G572&t=KJV; portal at http://www.eliyah.com/lexicon.html.

2. Michael Boehm, "What Is Grave Sucking?," Youth Apologetics Training, February 13, 2014, http://youthapologeticstraining.com/grave-sucking/.

3. David Jackman, *The Authentic Church: What Are Our Priorities Before Christ Comes Again?* (Fearn, Scotland: Christian Focus, 1998), 62.

4. Brian D. McLaren, *A Generous Orthodoxy* (Grand Rapids, MI: Zondervan, 2004), 35.

5. Paul F. Knitter, *Without Buddha I Could Not Be a Christian* (London: Oneworld Publications, 2009), 103.

6. Ibid., 95.

7. Francis A. Schaeffer, *The Great Evangelical Disaster* (Wheaton, IL: Crossway, 1984), 141 (emphasis in the original).

Chapter 3: The Barbarian Invasion

1. Compiled from: Von J. Rosenkranz, T. Röthemeier, and A. Wieberneit, "Es War Gruselig, Niemand Hat Uns Geholfen," *Bild*, January 6, 2016, http://www.bild.de /regional/hamburg/hamburg/es-war-gruselig-niemand-hat-uns-geholfen-44034422 .bild.html (translated by Google); Alison Smale, "As Germany Welcomes Migrants, Sexual Attacks in Cologne Point to a New Reality," *New York Times*, January 14, 2016, http://www.nytimes.com/2016/01/15/world/europe/as-germany-welcomes -migrantssexual-attacks-in-cologne-point-to-a-new-reality.html?_r=3; BBC, "Germany Shocked by Cologne New Year Gang Assaults on Women," BBC.com, January 5, 2016, http://www.bbc.com/news/world-europe-35231046; Ellie Flynn, "'I Was Groped Between My Legs': More Brave Victims from Cologne Sex Assaults Describe Horror as 2000 Strong Mob Attacked," *Sun*, January 7, 2016, https://www.thesun.co.uk/archives /news/53743/i-was-groped-between-my-legs-more-brave-victims-from-cologne-sex -assaults-describe-horror-as-2000-strong-mob-attacked/.

2. Scott Greer, "The Migrant Rape Culture the Political Elite Wishes Were Fake," *Daily Caller*, January 6, 2016, http://dailycaller.com/2016/01/06/the-migrant-rape-culture -political-elites-wishes-were-fake/.

3. Shamil Shams, "Opinion: Cologne attacks on Muslims show incompatibility of cultures," DW.com, January 11, 2016, http://www.dw.com/en/opinion-cologne-attacks -on-muslims-show-incompatibility-of-cultures/a-18971622.

4. Emma-Kate Symons, "Cologne attacks: 'This Is Sexual Terrorism Directed Towards Women,'" Women in the World, in association with the *New York Times,* January 19, 2016, http://nytlive.nytimes.com/womenintheworld/2016/01/19/cologne-attacks -this-is-sexual-terrorism-directed-towards-women/.

5. Ibid.

6. Evan Andrews, "8 Reasons Why Rome Fell," History.com, January 14, 2014, http://www.history.com/news/history-lists/8-reasons-why-rome-fell.

7. Ibid.

8. Will Durant and Ariel Durant, *The Story of Civilization*, vol. 3, *Caesar and Christ: A History of Roman Civilization and of Christianity from Their Beginnings to A.D. 325* (New York: Simon & Schuster, 1944), 366.

9. Edward McNall Burns, *Western Civilizations: Their History and Their Culture* (New York: Norton, 1968), 237.

10. Salvian, *The Writings of Salvian, the Presbyter*, Fathers of the Church Patristic Series, trans. Jeremiah F. O'Sullivan (Washington, D.C.: Catholic University Press, 1947), 193–94, 222.

11. Niall Ferguson, "Complexity and Collapse: Empires on the Edge of Chaos," *Foreign Affairs*, March/April 2010, http://www.foreignaffairs.com/articles/65987/niall -ferguson/complexity-and-collapse.

12. Zosimus, *New History*, bk. 5 (London: Green and Chaplin, 1814), http://www .tertullian.org/fathers/zosimus05_book5.htm.

13. Bradford Richardson, "LGBT Activists Blame Christians for Orlando Attack," *Washington Times*, June 13, 2016, http://www.washingtontimes.com/news/2016/jun/13/activists-blame-christians-orlando-attack/.
14. Editorial Board, "The Corrosive Politics That Threaten L.G.B.T. Americans," *New York Times*, June 15, 2016, http://www.nytimes.com/2016/06/15/opinion/the-corrosive-politics-that-threaten-lgbt-americans.html?_r=0.
15. William Watkinson, "ISIS Extremists Execute a Gay Man by Throwing Him off a Building, Say Activists," *International Business Times*, July 23, 2016, http://www.ibtimes.co.uk/isis-extremists-execute-gay-man-by-throwing-him-off-building-say-activists-1572154.

Chapter 4: The City of Man and the City of God
1. Michael Burger, ed., *Sources for the History of Western Civilization*, vol. 1, *From Antiquity to the Mid-Eighteenth Century*, 2nd ed. (Toronto: University of Toronto Press, 2015), 239.

Chapter 5: Choices That Change History
1. Rachel Cooke, "Living with Anxiety: Britain's Silent Epidemic," *Guardian* (UK), September 14, 2013, https://www.theguardian.com/society/2013/sep/15/anxiety-epidemic-gripping-britain.
2. Will Hutton, "Only Fundamental Social Change Can Defeat the Anxiety Epidemic," *Guardian* (UK), May 7, 2016, https://www.theguardian.com/global/commentisfree/2016/may/07/mental-health-policy-anxiety-natasha-devon-young-people.

Chapter 6: A Dividing Wall of Enmity
1. The Venerable Bede, *On Genesis*, trans. Calvin B. Kendall (Liverpool, UK: Liverpool University Press, 2008), 140.
2. Geoffrey W. Bromiley, ed., *The International Standard Bible Encyclopedia* (Grand Rapids: MI, Eerdmans, 1986), 4:546.

Chapter 7: Confusion and Collapse
1. Louise Mensch, "Exclusive: France 'Suppressed Reports of Gruesome Torture' at Bataclan Massacre," Heat Street, July 15, 2016, http://heatst.com/uk/exclusive-france-suppressed-news-of-gruesome-torture-at-bataclan-massacre/.
2. Jonah Bennett, "French Prime Minister on Nice Terror Attack: 'France Is Going to Have to Live with Terrorism,'" Daily Caller, July 15, 2016, http://dailycaller.com/2016/07/15/french-prime-minister-on-nice-terror-attack-france-is-going-to-have-to-live-with-terrorism/.
3. Rory Mulholland, "Normandy Jihadists Smiled at Nuns as They Slaughtered Priest," *Telegraph*, July 30, 2016, http://www.telegraph.co.uk/news/2016/07/30/normandy-jihadists-smiled-at-nuns-as-they-slaughtered-priest/.

4. Fr. Mark A. Pilon, "Religious Blindness—and its Consequences—for Europe," *The Catholic Thing* (blog), July 27, 2016, https://www.thecatholicthing.org/2016/07/27 /religious-blindness-and-its-consequences-for-europe/.

5. Ibid.

6. Ibid.

Chapter 8: The Pattern of Babylon

1. Shelby Grad and David Colker, "Nancy Reagan Turned to Astrology in White House to Protect Her Husband," *Los Angeles Times*, March 6, 2016, http://www.latimes.com /local/lanow/la-me-ln-nancy-reagan-astrology-20160306-story.html.

2. Soeren Kern, "Meet the First Muslim Mayor of London," Gatestone Institute International Policy Council, May 8, 2016, https://www.gatestoneinstitute.org/8011 /sadiq-khan.

3. Raheem Kassam and Oliver Lanes, "London's Iconic Red Buses to Declare 'Glory to Allah,'" Breitbart.com, May 2016, http://www.breitbart.com/london/2016/05/08 /london-buses-declare-glory-allah/.

Chapter 9: The Clash of Cultures

1. Lawrence Wright, The Looming Tower: Al-Qaeda and the Road to 9/11 (New York: Vintage, 2007), 36.

2. Drew Desilver, "World's Muslim Population More Widespread than You Might Think," Pew Research, June 7, 2013, http://www.pewresearch.org/fact-tank/2013/06/07/worlds -muslim-population-more-widespread-than-you-might-think/.

Chapter 10: Warning Signs of Impending Judgment

1. P. Jooste, "An Audience with the Queen," Marie-Stuart.co.uk, http://www.marie-stuart .co.uk/MaryvKnox.htm; the author has paraphrased some dialogue for the sake of clarity.

2. Mark Woods, "Scotland's Great Reformer: Who was John Knox?," ChristianToday.com, April 6, 2016, http://www.christiantoday.com/article/scotlands.great.reformer.who.was .john.knox/83454.htm.

3. John Witte and Frank S. Alexander, *The Teachings of Modern Protestantism on Law, Politics, and Human Nature* (New York: Columbia University Press, 2007), 246.

4. Aleksandr Solzhenitsyn, *Détente, Democracy, and Dictatorship*, 3rd ed. (New Brunswick, NJ: Transaction, 2009), 87.

5. Scott Hennen, *Grass Roots: A Commonsense Action Agenda for America* (New York: Simon & Schuster, 2011), 302.

6. Department of Justice, Office of Public Affairs, "U.S. Departments of Justice and Education Release Joint Guidance to Help Schools Ensure the Civil Rights of Transgender Students," news release, May 13, 2016, https://www.justice.gov/opa/pr /us-departments-justice-and-education-release-joint-guidance-help-schools-ensure -civil-rights.

Chapter 11: The Hope for a New Reformation

1. Glenn Sunshine, "Chiune Sugihara (1900-1986)," *BreakPoint* (blog), February 18, 2013, http://www.colsoncenter.org/the-center/columns/call-response/19313-christians-who-changed-their-world.

2. Martin Luther King Jr., "I've Been to the Mountaintop," Mason Temple (Church of God in Christ Headquarters), Memphis, Tennessee, April 3, 1968, AmericanRhetoric.com, http://www.americanrhetoric.com/speeches/mlkivebeentothemountaintop.htm (minor changes in punctuation made by the author).

3. Thomas Jefferson, "Jefferson's Letter to the Danbury Baptists: The Final Letter, as Sent," Library of Congress, https://www.loc.gov/loc/lcib/9806/danpre.html.

4. Megan Hart, "Spring Lake's Christ Community Church Removes Cross, Changes Name to C3Exchange," *Muskegon Chronicle*, June 23, 2010, http://www.mlive.com/news/muskegon/index.ssf/2010/06/spring_lakes_christ_community.html.

5. Michelle D. Anderson, "Spring Lake Church Plans to Reinstall Controversial Cross Removed in 2010," MLive.com, January 23, 2013, http://www.mlive.com/news/muskegon/index.ssf/2013/01/muskegon_area_church_restores.html.

Chapter 12: Finding Our Way Home

1. Hollie McKay, "Confessions of a Captured ISIS Fighter," FoxNews.com, July 13, 2016, http://www.foxnews.com/world/2016/07/13/confessions-captured-isis-fighter.html.

2. Ann O'Neill, "The Reinvention of Ted Turner," CNN, November 17, 2013, http://www.cnn.com/2013/11/17/us/ted-turner-profile/.

3. Harry Vom Bruch, "Vital Truth Illustration," *Grace and Truth: A Bible Study Magazine for Earnest Men and Women Everywhere*, January 1932–December 1932, https://archive.org/stream/gracetruth19clif_9/gracetruth19clif_9_djvu.txt. (Some quotes altered for clarity.)

ABOUT THE AUTHOR

MICHAEL YOUSSEF, PhD, is the founder and president of Leading The Way with Dr. Michael Youssef, a worldwide ministry that leads the way for people living in spiritual darkness to discover the light of Christ through the creative use of media and on-the-ground ministry teams. Daily, *Leading The Way* is sharing the gospel with the nations, broadcasting in multiple languages on radio and TV more than twelve thousand times a week to audiences across six continents. Dr. Youssef is also the founding pastor of The Church of The Apostles in Atlanta, Georgia.

IF YOU ENJOYED THIS BOOK, WILL YOU CONSIDER SHARING THE MESSAGE WITH OTHERS?

Mention the book in a blog post or through Facebook, Twitter, Pinterest, or upload a picture through Instagram.

Recommend this book to those in your small group, book club, workplace, and classes.

Head over to facebook.com/worthypublishing, "LIKE" the page, and post a comment as to what you enjoyed the most.

Tweet "I recommend reading #TheBarbariansAreHere by @MichaelAYoussef // @worthypub"

Pick up a copy for someone you know who would be challenged and encouraged by this message.

Write a book review online.

WORTHY®
PUBLISHING

Visit us at worthypublishing.com

twitter.com/worthypub

worthypub.tumblr.com

facebook.com/worthypublishing

pinterest.com/worthypub

instagram.com/worthypub

youtube.com/worthypublishing